D0358872

cucina siciliana

AUTHENTIC RECIPES AND CULINARY SECRETS FROM SICILY

CLARISSA HYMAN
PHOTOGRAPHY BY PETER CASSIDY

conran
OCTOPUS

Dedication
For my mother and father

First published in 2002 by Conran Octopus Limited, a part of Octopus Publishing Group, 2–4 Heron Quays, London E14 4JP
www.conran-octopus.co.uk
Reprinted in 2003

The publisher would like to thank Peter Cassidy for the use of the photographs on pages 2–3, 27 left and right, 30, 136 above and below, 147 left and right.

British Cataloguing-in-Publication Data.
A catalogue record for this book is available from the British Library
ISBN 1 84091 183 2

Publishing Director Lorraine Dickey
Editorial Cookery Consultant Jenni Muir
Commissioning Editor Bridget Hopkinson
Senior Editor Muna Reyal
Copy Editor Marion Moisy

Creative Director Leslie Harrington
Art Editor Megan Smith
Photography Peter Cassidy
Food Stylist Maxine Clark
Stylist Róisín Nield
Map illustrator Russell Bell

Production Director Zoe Fawcett
Senior Production Controller Manjit Sihra

Printed and bound in China

contents

Introduction

Red. Blood red. Earth red. Orange red.

The thousand shades of red in a pile of tomatoes laid out to dry under an inflamed sun. Red and yellow, the colours of Sicily. Yellow for the vast fields of wheat in empty, feudal landscapes; yellow for the saffron of ancient Greece; for acid-yellow lemons and molten honey from golden beehives.

Sicilian colours and food have an intensity and brilliance that overwhelm the senses. The three-cornered island, lapped by three different seas, is where Europe stops and Africa begins. Poor little Sicily, forever destined to be kicked into the middle of the Mediterranean Sea by the big boot of Italy; it partially explains why the rest of Italy was once referred to as the *continente*. Sicily is another country. One that has been blessed, and cursed.

Such is the fertility of the land, Greek hunting dogs were said to lose the trail when the spring flowers were in bloom. The lush, productive soil and plentiful seas, plus Sicily's strategic position between competing spheres of interest, has always made the island an irresistible treasure to exploit. Not only has Sicily been invaded and occupied a dozen or more times over the centuries, but the island has also been devastated by volcanoes, earthquakes, floods and natural disasters of almost Biblical proportions. As a result, Sicilians have developed a complex siege mentality, an inward-looking, cunning and sometimes brutal, often cynically amusing cast of mind that places self, family and clan interest above the common good. The great journalist Luigi Barzini wrote in *The Italians*: 'If most Italians manage at times to weave skilfully in and out of written laws, most Sicilians appear to avoid them all completely.'

Contradictions and extremes abound in Sicily, they always have done. A place of both intense light and extreme darkness, Sicily can be seductive yet shocking, with stunning scenery and intrusive tower blocks, the most beautiful of Greek temples and eyesore, illegal buildings, Roman mosaics and brutally sited power stations, splendidly restored opera houses as well as forgotten Baroque masterpieces.

Except, in Sicily, nothing is ever quite as it seems; it needs a shift of perspective to understand that the incompleted houses littering the countryside are half-built, not half-abandoned, waiting to be finished and occupied when family fortunes permit. Or to understand that ugly new buildings in ancient hilltop towns are civic symbols of success, pointers to the future, not the past. And you need to think Sicilian to understand why many are happy to have Mafia chiefs live in their neighbourhood – a way of deterring trouble, they reason, rather than encouraging it. 'Better the trouble you already know, than the good still to come,' goes the despairing, cynical proverb.

Vicious circles of oppression, corruption, foreign rule, high taxes, emigration and family separation, absentee noble landlords, immense feudal estates, piracy and bandits, vanishing subsidies, unemployment, power politics and dubious deals – all have, in the past, paralysed the forces of progress. In the kitchen, however, this inertia and resistance to change has also enabled the survival of domestic dishes and ingredients that offer comfort and stability in a hostile, threatening world.

Sicilian cooking is living history, its gastronomy born out of serial rape. Each wave of conquest has helped shape the Sicilian table. The Greeks came bearing gifts of honey, wine, ricotta and olives, followed by the rapacious Roman cultivators of wheat, grains and pulses. After invasion by the Vandals, a return to Greek Byzantine rule gave a considerable boost to local agriculture with the establishment of a number of monasteries across the island, bringing with them a taste for sharp cheeses and spicy biscuits.

Cianciana (top right), Monte Cófano (bottom right)

Tiled column at Monreale (left), Stone column at Selinunte (right)

In the first century, the Arabs (North African Berbers and Spanish Moslems, all called Saracens by the Sicilians) transformed the island's culinary composition with the introduction of sugar cane, citrus fruits, aubergines, rice, spices, tuna traps and an ingenious system of irrigation. They also introduced stuffed vegetables, cuscus, deep-frying and spit-roasting. Their influence was perpetuated by the Jewish trading communities that remained in Sicily after the Saracens departed, until expelled to the Italian mainland by the Spanish Inquisition. The Normans, in turn, left a legacy of dried fish and blue-eyed children, and the Angevins, in the 13th century, brought sweet shortcrust pastry, *farsumagru* (stuffed meat roll), eel with spices and bechamel sauce.

Tomatoes, potatoes, peppers, squash and chocolate came with the 400 years of Aragonese and Spanish rule, along with a love of florid decoration, an acute awareness of appearances, and a glut of aristocratic titles. This is recorded in the ostentatious architecture of the Sicilian Baroque and in every swirl on a cassata cake. The Spanish also introduced the prickly pear from the New World, a fruit that has embedded itself so well into the Sicilian soil and soul, it has become a symbol of the island. In turn, Piedmontese, Hapsburg and Bourbon rule all played a part in the Sicilian kitchen; even the brief English presence is remembered in the legacy of Marsala wine.

From earliest times, there has been a distinction in Sicily between the food of the rich and poor. While the Sicilian plebs under the Greeks and Romans ate little more than gruel, cities such as Syracuse and Agrigento became renowned for their fabulous banquets. *Cucina baronale*, established in noble kitchens by medieval and Renaissance times, was heightened by the arrival of the Spanish aristocracy on the island, lavish and profligate while the majority of peasants faced near starvation.

Spanish influence gave way to French fashion in the 18th century, when the great aristocratic houses took their lead from sophisticated, cutting-edge French cuisine. *Monzù* master-chefs (a corruption of the French

Fountain in Cefalù (left), Walkway at Monreale (right)

monsieur) added extra refinement of technique and rich ingredients, such as butter, cream and brandy, to the already elaborate *cucina baronale*, introducing complex pies and pasta timbales, galantines and the like.

La cucina povera has remained dependant on the basic ingredients, many of which are found elsewhere around the Mediterranean. In Sicily, however, the flavours seem more powerful, hotter, spicier, sweeter, their simplicity elevated by the sheer quality of the natural produce that thrives under the southern sun. Not just flavour: colours, scent and size seem exaggerated and intensified. As both Barzini and Goethe understood, Sicily is Italy magnified, every quality and defect of the national psyche writ larger than life. The same is true of the cooking.

The staples of bread and oil, pasta and tomatoes, fish and fruit are fired by the use of anchovies, hot pepper, basil, mint, fennel, oregano, citrus, almonds and pistachios as well as the classic combinations of capers and green olives, pine nuts and currants, and vinegar and honey. The wonder is that such a tutti-frutti tapestry of heady elements does not become totally incoherent. Instead, Sicilian cooking, full of scent and colour mixed with over-the-top exuberance, is vigorous and expressive, a melting-pot gastronomy born out of an innate, slow-simmering understanding of possibilities.

Poverty, absolute, extreme and degrading, has ironically been a stimulus for the Sicilian housewife to improvise a little something out of a lot of nothing, to work in kitchens without the luxury of an oven or to make one egg feed four mouths. 'There is no better sauce than hunger,' goes an old proverb.

Sicilians, especially the strong, feisty Sicilian women, have fought hard to do the best for their children, driven by hunger to heights of remarkable inventiveness. In the Sicilian kitchen, nothing is ever wasted: the peelings from vegetables can go to make *polpette* (little balls of meat, chicken, fish or vegetables), or a wonderful dish of pasta can be made with garlic, oil and chilli peppers alone. Even bread must be valued down to the last crumb.

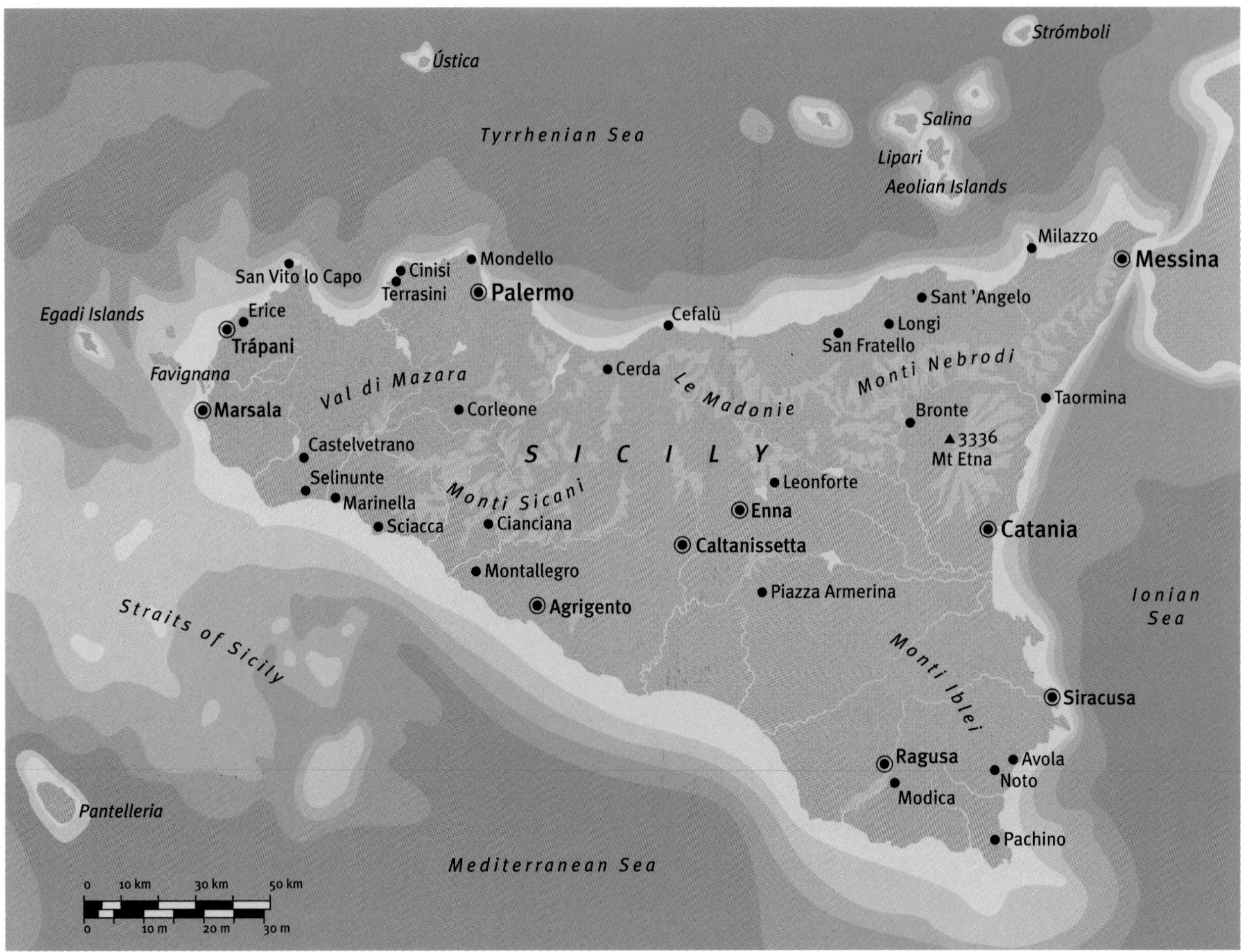

Intense hunger is seared in the collective memory, and old habits die hard, even with the island's greatly improved standard of living.

Superstition and religion still go hand in hand. Traditional dishes are tied to the extensive Sicilian calendar of festivals and saints' days celebrated with ancient ritual, processions, songs, dances, stupefying re-enactments, decorations and extraordinary acts of devotion, from living nativity scenes to floats pulled by a thousand barefooted people, weeping plaster saints and miracle-working relics.

Pithy Sicilian humour, expressive wordplay and instinct for drama have also enriched daily life. Dishes with dialect names such as *pasta chi sardi a 'mmari* (pasta with the sardines still in the sea), or *pasta du'malu tempu* (bad weather pasta, for when the fishermen were unable to go out on their boats), are bittersweet and poignant. However the Sicilians also have an irrepressible talent for vivid vulgarisms that has resulted in a whole genre of dishes called pregnant buns, virgins' breasts, nuns' thighs, angels' pricks, hens' turds and, the earthiest of the lot, *lasagni cacati* (faeces lasagne), a broad, wavy pasta with minced meat traditionally served at New Year.

Despite the extreme Sicilian sweet tooth, much of the cooking is disarmingly straightforward, fresh and seasonal. Sicilian agriculture is recovering from decades of low investment, and comes too late for those who have abandoned the land, but the link remains strong and home-grown food is still appreciated. Everyone has a relative or friend with tomato plants or olive groves, a lemon tree, some vines or a row of vegetables, and throughout the island, seasonal produce is sold at street corners from the back of little three-wheeled trucks.

The first question a Sicilian asks when shopping is not 'How much?' but 'How fresh?' Most of the recipes in this book are almost subversively simple, but they are still dependent on ingredients of singular quality that can speak for themselves without a plateful of extraneous clutter. A few others, usually festive or party dishes, are as full of subtle layers as Sicilian society itself.

Everyone's home cooking, almost by definition, is always the best. Insular is an understatement. Many Sicilians remain unaware or dismissive of dishes, producers and traditions in other parts of the island: 'They don't know how to make it the way we do,' is a frequent refrain. 'They don't grow things as well as we do, our cheese is better, our oil finer, our bread best... ' but the converse of this culinary distrust is a chauvinistic pride in their own food and cooking that is enviable in today's mass-market world.

The terminology of Sicilian cooking, however, can be bewildering, with the same dish having different names, or the same name applied to different dishes depending on the region. In addition, every household has its variations on a basic theme, with small changes of ingredient or technique – the size of the cubed aubergine, the thickness of a tomato sauce, the colour of cooked onions – sanctified by time and custom. The recipes in this book are, for the most part, traditional, in the sense that they are a snapshot of family food cooked in a certain way in a certain place at a certain time, but there are no strict rules. Sicilian cooking is not suspended in time, and recipes evolve as modern Sicilians incorporate non-traditional ingredients and shortcuts such as food processors, frozen peas and even bought-in tomato sauce without notable loss of quality.

The result is always consumed with a philosophy that is direct – if something tastes good, they argue, why should you want anything else? And they taste and enjoy with remarkable *joie de vivre*, eating with a lusty, lip-smacking vigour, attacking the food without pretensions. Perhaps it's a plenty-to-eat-if-you're-quick mentality, or the folk memory of times when food, any food, was a luxury, or simply the understanding that food must be eaten at its moment of perfection. When the pasta comes to the table, all conversation and shouting cease.

There has been more change, however, in the past two decades, arguably, than in the past two centuries. The isolation of the interior, now criss-crossed by spectacular motorways, and the most rigid of social mores are both eroding. The cultural isolation of the island from the rest of Europe is diminishing as Sicily finally confronts the problems of organised crime. A new Sicily is emerging with new aspirations, and with it comes the post-modern success symbols of burger joints and ostrich farms, the irresistible lure of kiwifruit, canned sweetcorn and frozen samosas. Someone remarked to me that the biggest symbol of change in their lifetime was the availability of pet food on the supermarket shelves, in itself another major change in the way Sicilians are starting to shop, along with the inexorable slide to processed and industrialised foodstuffs. Sicily is long used to absorbing the influences of other lands on its cooking but this final assault on its individualism may be the last stand. Many of the small producers chronicled in this book are battling to keep alive the old methods of production before they are finally lost forever.

The Sicilian language has no future tense (indicative of a people who could only look back in despair, never forward with hope) and no word for privacy. Many Sicilian cookbooks automatically assume you are cooking for a small army, recipes for a hundred biscuits are not uncommon. Eating well is not just taken seriously, it is a social affair; meals may be simple and quick to prepare but they are not to be rushed. Food is an expression of Sicilian affection and hospitality, both of which can be quite engulfing. Initial suspicions allayed, introductions effected, I have rarely encountered such spontaneous generosity and kindness as I have in Sicily.

The last word on the subject goes to my friend Rosy's mamma, Signora Fillipa Bartolotta, ex-Michigan and now resident of Cinisi, who insisted: 'Tell them, if they want good food, they should come to Sicilia!' I told, them, Signora Bartolotta. I told them real good.

Clarissa Hyman, England, 2002

Sicilian meals

Before any Sicilian who sees this book protests they never eat fruit in the morning or have pasta at night, let me admit to a degree of arbitrariness in the structure. Every Sicilian, of course, is the exception that proves the rule but the fact is the familiar rhythm of the culinary week is changing as the meals that once provided the punctuation for family life start to shift. Most people still take their main meal at midday, eating only lightly in the evening, but the format is breaking up round the edges, particularly in the cities, especially as more women go out to work.

The structure of the book, therefore, tries to do two things – reflect a sense of the ebb and flow of the Sicilian day through an existing meal pattern, while filtering this through the needs of more contemporary lifestyles. The main guidelines I have followed are to suggest sweet things for the morning, main-course ideas for lunchtime, savoury snacks for the afternoon and lighter meals for the evening. Naturally, any dish can be made for any meal – so, have pasta for lunch alone or grill fish for supper, eat sfinciuni at midmorning and cake in the afternoon, as you choose.

The classic Sicilian breakfast remains an espresso and a cornetto, a ubiquitous sweet croissant often filled with preserves or pastry cream. Brioche-style buns are topped with a dollop of granita and whipped cream in the summer. In their book *Sicilian Cookery*, Giuseppe and Palmina Risicato describe the favourite breakfast enjoyed by Dr Costa, the local doctor in Vizzini, as 'a biscuit, a cigar and a glass of Cognac'.

Pranzo means a large meal of some importance, generally taken at lunchtime although it could equally be later in the day. *Cena* refers to the evening meal, usually a light supper. Meals sometimes begin with *antipasti* ('to undress the appetite'), although this is a relatively new concept in Sicily and mostly served in restaurants rather than the home. Antipasto dishes were once just little extra dishes to bolster a main course or were *tornagusto* on the tables of the wealthy, dishes intended to refresh the palate in between courses. Most *paesani*, however, needed no encouragement to whet appetites already sharpened by hours of laborious work in the fields; even now, most Sicilians simply want a plate of pasta with no preliminaries and are happy to eat it day or night, with or without a subsequent course.

Whether taken at lunch or in the evening, the main meal of the day usually includes a substantial portion of soup, pasta or rice, followed by a smaller serving of fish or meat, served alone on the plate. Any vegetable or salad usually comes on a separate plate or side dish. Unless it is a meal of special significance, dessert is almost invariably fresh fruit.

Midmorning and midafternoon are the time for snacks, sweet and savoury, to break up the hours between the main meals, and pacify any little pockets of hunger remaining in the stomach. Many sweet dishes come into their own at this time. Sicilians can put away remarkable quantities of cakes and pastries at any time of the morning, and repeat the exercise in the afternoon. Ice cream is eaten morning, noon and night, for breakfast and for late night snacks as well.

Spuntini are generally midmorning snacks, while *merende* are taken in the afternoon, but the boundaries blur and the division of dishes is often unclear. Still, everyone understands the concept of a little something to eat, *qualche cosa da mangiare*, whether it's a slice of pizza, a plate of olives, piece of cheese or the endless amounts of roasted chickpeas and salted pumpkin seeds obsessively consumed when Sicilians are out strolling for the evening *passeggiata*.

Food, whenever eaten, remains a central theme of Sicilian life. As an old proverb says: 'With a contented stomach, your heart is forgiving, with an empty stomach, you forgive nothing.'

'With a contented stomach, your heart is forgiving, with an empty stomach, you forgive nothing.' SICILIAN PROVERB

Ingredients

ALMONDS

Almonds should be used as fresh as possible, stored in a tightly sealed jar in a cool, dry place as they become rancid quickly. To skin almonds, blanch them briefly in boiling water, drain and squeeze each one so they simply pop out of their skins. To toast almonds, preheat the oven to 180°C/350°F/Gas 4, place in a single layer on a baking sheet and bake for 10 minutes.

ANCHOVIES

Whole anchovies packed in salt keep well in the fridge, covered with foil or plastic wrap. Before using, make sure the salt is soft and white and not discoloured. Wash thoroughly in cold water, then run your thumbnail along the spine and pull out the bony little skeleton. Behead also, if necessary. Otherwise, buy salted fillets, soaking them well in water before use, or buy the best quality anchovies packed in olive oil you can find. If very salty, soak in milk for 10 minutes before using. Anchovies in oil, once opened, should be kept in a glass container in the fridge and covered with oil. When cooking with anchovies, always heat them very gently or they will become bitter.

AUBERGINES

There are two varieties used in Sicilian cooking: the club-like, shiny, deep purple 'Turkish' variety, sometimes called *nostrano*, and the small, round, mauve and white streaked 'Tunisian' aubergine usually preferred for its sweeter, fresher flavour. Sicilians also distinguish between male and female aubergines. Then, there is the ongoing debate over whether to salt or not to salt. Most modern varieties of aubergine do not need salting to eliminate bitterness, but to lessen the amount of oil they would otherwise absorb.

BREADCRUMBS

In Sicily, all leftover bread goes to make breadcrumbs, an essential ingredient in Sicilian cooking, for coating, stuffing, binding and even sprinkling over pasta. Different breadcrumbs are used for different purposes.

Pangrattato: coarsely grated or processed breadcrumbs made from stale bread, including the crust. In Sicily, the bread is bagged and hung from an outdoors rafter for several days to dry out in the heat. Elsewhere, *pangrattato* can often be found ready-made in Italian delis that cater to the requirements of the local Italian community. It keeps well in an airtight container stored in a cool, dry place. A more refined version uses only the stale white part of the bread, slowly dried out in the oven, then grated and sieved to produce a very fine crumb.

Pangrattato alle erbe: seasoned breadcrumbs that are used to cover fish, meat and vegetables or as stuffings and toppings. To make them, mix breadcrumbs with two-thirds the amount of grated pecorino cheese, dried oregano, chopped fresh parsley, salt and some chopped garlic, if wished. The breadcrumbs can be stored (without adding the parsley and garlic) for two or three weeks in a tightly closed container in the fridge.

Mollica: *pangrattato* that has been browned in olive oil over a very low heat until lightly toasted. Keep turning it with a spatula to distribute the oil and watch it like a hawk: nothing seems to happen at first, then before you can say *uno, due, tre,* they're burnt. You can also add a little garlic. *Mollica* needs to be used the day it is made. Sprinkle it over roasted vegetables or use it instead of grated cheese with pasta.

CANDIED PEEL AND GLACÉ FRUIT

Look for good quality Italian imports of candied citron, lemon and orange peel. After Christmas they are often reduced in price. Store them in a cool place in a covered jar. Sicilian glacé fruit, mainly used for cake decoration, is harder to come by, but preserves intact the true flavour of the fruit underneath the sugar coating.

CAPERS

On the jagged, Moorish island of Pantelleria, summer home to Giorgio Armani, and on Salina, one of the volcanic Aeolian Islands, whose winds were created as a

Above from left: almonds, aubergine, capers, carob

parting gift to Odysseus from King Aeolus, capers grow wild. They burst out of chinks in stone walls, from cracks in rocky outcrops, their stubborn roots digging deep down search of moisture. The tangled, spiny bushes trail blue-green leaves and bear tight little buds that turn into abundant numbers of delicate but short-lived flowers that open in the morning and are gone by the afternoon.

Whether wild or cultivated, the hard, edible buds have to be hand-picked just as they reach the right size; it is arduous work, as the plant flowers continuously in summer and each has to be regularly revisited to catch the khaki buds before they open. Once picked, the large, flavoursome capers are dried out in the air and sun, then layered in salt brine to cure in barrels for a week, and turned daily to prevent softening.

After draining, they are packed in coarse sea salt, and it is a truth universally held by both islands that only salt can bring out the true flavour of the caper. They may challenge each other for the title of the best capers in Sicily (therefore the world), but the one thing they do agree upon is that to drown capers in vinegar is the equivalent of overcooking pasta: quite unthinkable.

Before using capers packed in salt, rinse them well in cold, running water, then drain and pat dry.

CAROB

Carob is found mostly around Ragusa. The old, Biblical evergreen grows wild on barren, stony land, each one an oasis of shelter for shepherds and peasants. The trees can also be cultivated as they need little care or nourishment. The leathery, mahogany pods are harvested in September and sun-dried. The velvety pulp is very sweet and the hard seeds were once used by jewellers to measure gold and precious stones, the original *carat* from the Greek *keration*. Most carob goes for animal feed, but it is also used in confectionery and as a cocoa substitute. Karrua are an enterprising new company near Modica specialising in carob products, including an excellent syrup.

CAULIFLOWER AND BROCCOLI

In western Sicily, cauliflower is called *broccolo* or *vrócculi*, while dark green broccoli is called *sparaceddi*. This can lead to some confusion, but in most recipes cauliflower and broccoli are interchangeable. In Sicily, you find white, purple and acid-green cauliflowers of immense girth and strong flavour. Romanesca, with bright green curd that grows in whorls, can also be used, or flowering broccoli.

CHEESE

The type of cheese used is often less important than its age, therefore it is not so much a question of direct substitution as deciding the function and context in which the cheese is to be used. For an elastic, easily melted, mild cheese try provolone dolce, and provolone picante for the same texture but with a stronger flavour, or failing that, mozzarella. Pecorino is the grating cheese of choice – use Sardo or Romano, if you can't find Siciliano. Parmigiano Reggiano is increasingly used

Above from left: squash, pasta, figs, pomegranates

as a status symbol. For ricotta dishes, use ewes' milk ricotta if you can find it, otherwise use a good-quality cows' milk ricotta.

CHESTNUTS

The village of Sant'Alfio, on the eastern side of Etna, is famous for the Chestnut Tree of One Hundred Horses. The ancient clump of trees, said to date from the 13th century, has a circumference of 52 m/172ft. The story goes that Queen Giovanna d'Angi and her escort of knights took shelter here one night from a sudden storm. The village has taken pride in the fact ever since. Use either dried Italian chestnuts, soaked overnight, or good quality cans of whole chestnuts or chestnut purée.

CHICKPEAS

Chickpeas play a notable part in Sicilian history. The hatred against the French conquerors and their heavy taxes exploded in 1282 in the incident known as the Sicilian Vespers. Nearly all the French in Sicily were massacred, summarily identified by their inability to correctly pronounce the unpronounceable (at least to a non-Sicilian) *ciciri*, the Sicilian word for chickpea. Either soak dried chickpeas in cold water overnight before boiling, or used canned ones.

COOKING FATS

All butter is unsalted, and the oil is always olive. Use extra virgin olive oil wherever possible, although pure olive oil or a good vegetable oil can be used for deep-frying. In Sicily lard was for centuries the most common cooking fat; butter was restricted to the nobility after the construction of a Crown Dairy in Partinico in the 19th century, and olive oil production, neglected under the Arabs, was not revived until the 18th century. Lard is used less today, but it does give an inimitable flavour and can be heated to high temperatures without smoking.

COURGETTES

These are less used in Sicily than might be assumed. Those commonly found in Britain are called *zucchine genovese* or *napoletana*, and generally used for stuffing or grilling, never pasta. More popular varieties of squash include summer *zucca* or *cucuzza lunga* (a long, light green squash with bland, white pulp that goes to make candied *zuccata* used in *pasticceria*), as well as *zucchina bianca di Sicilia*, which are like thick cucumbers, and *cucuzza cintinaria* or chayote. In autumn, large yellow-green pumpkins with orange flesh, called *zucca gialla*, are used to make sweet-and-sour pumpkin. Substitute whatever squash and pumpkin you can find.

Tenerumi are the shoots and young leaves of *cucuzza lunga*. They are said to be easily digestible, refreshing and light. An old saying goes, to eat pasta with *tenerumi* means to eat almost next to nothing.

EGGS

All eggs used in testing the recipes in this book were medium-sized, organic eggs. Always use eggs at room temperature, especially when whisking the whites.

Above from left: lemons, bell peppers, basil, chilli peppers

FLOUR

Unless specified, all flour used in this book's recipes is 00 Italian soft wheat flour.

FRUIT AND VEGETABLES

Many Sicilian recipes allow their ingredients to speak for themselves and are served as simply as possible. It is difficult to reproduce the essence of the sun that characterises most Sicilian fruit and vegetables, but you stand a fighting chance if you use organic produce or can find produce imported directly from Italy.

HERBS

Basil: Sicilian basil seems to have a powerful accent hothouse plants lack, but never use dried as a substitute for fresh. Use the leaves only, as the stems can make a dish bitter, and always tear the leaves, never cut them.
Bay leaves: one of the most widely used Sicilian herbs. Hot water with bay leaves and lemon peel is a popular remedy for all ills and ailments. Try to find fresh leaves, dried are a waste of money.
Mint: always use fresh mint, *Mentha spicata* or spearmint, although the flavour seems subdued compared to Sicilian mint. The balance of mint in any dish has to be carefully judged according to personal taste.
Oregano: in Sicily, *Origanum heracleoticum* grows wild in the mountains, the bunches gathered when it blooms in the summer, then hung up to dry. The name came with the Greeks (*oros* for mountain and *ganos* for splendour) for it was the healing herb found by Heracles when he descended to Hades. The pungent aroma of the herb is intensified by the Sicilian sun and is only ever used dried in cooking. Look for oregano dried on the branch or bring some back from Sicily.
Parsley: flat-leaved or Italian parsley has the best depth of flavour. Use it in preference to the curly kind.

MILK

All recipes in this book containing milk require whole milk, organic for preference.

PEPERONCINO AND BLACK PEPPER

Many Sicilians consider black pepper to be unhealthy and prefer to season their food with hot red pepper flakes or peperoncino. You can use peperoncino ground or, as I prefer, in flakes. Go cautiously at first – you will find that tolerance soon builds and food tastes bland without the little jolt it provides. Sicilians use it in cooking or have a shaker or bowl on the table.

In place of peperoncino you can add a small, whole dried chilli to your dish or, alternatively, infuse a jar of olive oil with chilli peppers and leave it to stand for a few weeks before using, a drop or two at a time. Be warned, though, it gets hotter the longer it is left. If you opt for black pepper instead, always grind it freshly.

PINE NUTS AND CURRANTS

Memories of the Moorish occupation live on in the extensive use of pine nuts or *pinoli* in Sicilian cooking. The nuts, from ancient trees shaped like lofty umbrellas,

Above from left: prickly pear plant and fruit, tomatoes

can be harvested only when the large cones that contain them are completely open. They are protected by a hard shell that needs to be cracked open in order to release the creamy white kernel – one reason for their high cost.

The mixture of pine nuts and small black currants (from Corinth grapes) is known as *passoli e pinoli* and frequently sold ready-mixed in packets, although the percentage of nuts to fruit is often suspiciously low.

PRICKLY PEARS

An immigrant from the Americas that has become emblematic of the island, *Fichi d'India* or Indian figs grow profusely in the wild, their strange, glowing fruit tempting and forbidding at the same time. They look like neon hand-grenades, varying in shade from greeny-gold to pink, purple, red and almost off-white, but colour is no guide to flavour. The two cultivated varieties, *bastarduni* and *surfarina*, are particularly large, have fewer seeds and reveal fruit of stunning, jewel-like colour that is refreshing and sugary. Gathering the fruit is tricky, because of the profusion of nasty little spines. Once picked, these are rubbed off and rinsed away, a skilled task now done by machine. Even so, it is best to tackle prickly pears with a knife and fork; restaurants usually serve them peeled. The seeds are edible, but like leadshot.

SAFFRON

Use good quality saffron strands. Soak them in hot water, then add with the soaking liquid to the dish.

SALT

Always use sea salt, even if it's not from Trapani.

SUGAR

All the sugar used in these recipes is either caster or icing sugar. Sicilians have a very sweet tooth, and although the amounts have been reduced in many recipes from the originals, you may need to alter them even further according to personal preference.

TOMATOES

Buy well-ripened tomatoes, or leave them to ripen out of the fridge before using. Alternatively, use good Italian canned tomatoes, preferably organic. It makes a lot of difference to the final taste of the dish. Outside Sicily, the local speciality tomato extract *'strattu* is hard to find, so substitute twice the amount of concentrated tomato paste from a tube, sachet or can.

WATER

Many Sicilians still get their drinking water from public fountains that are fed directly from mountain springs. They refuse to drink tap water, but may condescend to cook with it. They could buy bottled water, but then why pay when you can get it free? Carlo Middione writes about his mother's fish stew made with rainwater in pre-acid rain times, and stresses that good-tasting water really makes a difference in cooking. If you live in a hard water area, or one with a high chlorine level, consider using the bottled stuff for special occasions.

Sicilian cheese

Despite encroaching industrialisation, Sicilian cheeses still reflect the season, the pasture, the milk and the maker. The survival of these cheeses, mostly unknown outside of Sicily, is increasingly under threat, but for the present, at least, they still represent what the shepherds once called *il frutto*, the fruit of the milk.

RICOTTA

Ricotta: should be eaten *freschissima*, as close as possible, they say, to its place of production, as each passing kilometre and hour diminishes its fragrance. A fresh dairy product rather than a cheese, ricotta literally means 'recooked' and is made from the whey left over from the making of other cheeses.

Ricotta salata: ricotta that has been drained in woven baskets, salted and dried in the sun for several weeks.

Ricotta infornata: ricotta drained in woven baskets then transferred to a greased pottery container. It is sprinkled with pepper and baked in a wood-fired oven until the exterior chars but the inside is sweet and slightly smoky.

PASTA FILATA

This group of cheeses is colloquially referred to as *caciocavallo* – the word derives from an ancient technique of hanging cheeses from poles, as if over a horse's back. Pasta filata means that the curd, immersed in hot water, is pulled or stretched. Mozzarella is the most famous non-Sicilian example.

Ragusano DOP: massive ingots of this golden cheese cascade down from ceilings, strung together with knotted cord, as if in the counting house of a fairytale giant. It is one of the most extraordinary sights in the cheesemaking world, known and prized since the 14th century. Made from unpasteurised cows' milk, the best comes from the milk of the rare Modicana breed, unique to Ragusa province. It requires great physical strength to shape the curd into the moulds, as each *scaluni* or step can weigh 10-16kg/22-33lb each. As they mature, oil and vinegar are rubbed periodically into the rind, producing a rind as polished as the steps of Modica's magnificent Baroque Cathedral. The paste is soft and mild, but the flavour intensifies as the cheese hardens and ages.

Caciocavallo Palermitano: made from unpasteurised cows' milk, this cheese is square, with an amber crust and straw-coloured paste. Smaller, oval-shaped ones are called Vastedda Palermitana.

Provola: a younger and more supple cheese with a distinctive pear shape. It is made from cows' milk and varies in shape from pendulous monsters to pert little numbers with pronounced nipples. One of the best is made in Floresta (925 inhabitants at the last count) in the Nebrodi mountains.

Vastedda della Valle del Belice: one of the very few pasta filata cheeses in Italy that is made with ewes' milk, courtesy of the indigenous breed of long-haired Belice sheep. The flat, ivory disc needs to be eaten fresh and has a superb, tangy but pure taste.

Caci Figurati: a charming curiosity, this cheese is made in the Nebrodi and Madonie mountains, fashioned into the shape of horses and fawns.

PASTA PRESSATA

This term means hard-pressed, semi-cooked cheese.

Pecorino Siciliano DOP: in *The Odyssey*, Homer recounts how the giant Polyphemus ate whey for supper in his Sicilian cave, surrounded by baskets of cheese. Still made from raw ewes' milk, pecorino is matured in underground cellars or caves for at least four months, and the rind bears the imprint of the rush basket in which it was drained. The white paste is compact and when mature has a strong, sharp taste, with echoes of mountain herbs. It is sometimes made with black peppercorns or peperoncino; there is also a trendy new generation of flavours such as rocket, sun-dried tomato, walnuts and pistachio. Pecorino is called *tuma* when very creamy, fresh and unsalted, *primosale* when newly salted, and *stagionato* when mature. Note that these terms are sometimes applied to other cheeses to indicate age and degree of maturation.

Canestrato: used as part-payment for tithes in the 15th century, canestrato takes its name from the rush basket in which it is drained. The tall, cylindrical cheese is made from a mix of cow and sheep's milk. Sweet when young, it sharpens and becomes more pungent as it ages.

Maiorchino: every Carnival, the shepherds of the small medieval hill towns of Basico and Novara in Messina compete to roll the matured cheeses down the steep streets. Maiorchino is made from raw ewes' milk, sometimes mixed with goats' milk, but is on the verge of extinction. Production is laborious. Before salting, the cheese is carefully pierced with olive wood or iron needles. They say you can taste the windfall chestnuts on which the sheep grazed.

Piacentino: an ancient, saffron-flavoured sheep's milk cheese studded with peppercorns from landlocked Enna. The name might derive from *piangentinu* – that which weeps – as the cheese, eaten relatively young, literally oozes moisture as it matures. This is collected in terracotta jugs and rubbed back into the cheese. Alternatively, the term might simply come from the word *piacere*, to please.

Fiore Sicano: a raw cows' milk cheese with an unusual, grey mould rind. It is made in the mountains straddling the provinces of Palermo and Agrigento.

Shepherd and flock, Cianciana

Sicilian wine

Sicilian wine has come of age. Although the island is awash with wine (if Sicily was a separate country, it would rank sixth in the world for wine production) for many years the island's vast output went for cheap bulk wine, sold in tanks and shipped out to be anonymously blended for mass consumption. Apart from a few admirable exceptions such as Corvo and Regaleali, the image of Sicilian wine was generally undistinguished. A case of quantity over quality.

But things have changed rapidly in the past few years. Young producers are setting their sights high, and the island's potential for wine greatness has begun to attract investment and attention from the rest of Italy. The move into fine wine by the giant Settesoli co-operative in Menfi also is a significant marker.

The Italian food and wine magazine *Gambero Rosso*, in a survey of Sicilian wine, attributes these major changes to the fact that land and vineyards in Sicily are reasonably priced, that EU laws on planting new vines make Sicily a favourable zone to buy into, and that good wine can be made there with relative ease. It points out the need for further improvement, such as a better balance between white and red grapes, but adds that native varieties such as Nero d'Avola, Inzolia and Grecanico are gaining ground. At the same time, endless sunshine, a virtual guarantee of successful growing, has meant that 'Chardonnay, Merlot and Cabernet Sauvignon do very well in this climate, which has led to comparisons between Sicily and California.' It's a dream held by many that may soon become a reality.

DOC WINES

There are 17 Sicilian DOC wines, amongst them:

Alcamo or Bianco Alcamo: a dry white from western Sicily made from Catarratto Bianco.

Cerasuolo di Vittoria: light red wine from Calabrese and Frappato grapes grown in southeast Sicily.

Contessa Entellina: wines grown in the Belice valley. Varietals must contain 85 per cent of the grape named.

Eloro: from the southeast, around Noto and Pachino.

Etna: a wide range of wines grown on volcanic soil.

Faro: a revival of a once-celebrated red from Messina.

Menfi: from Menfi and Sciacca, on the western coast.

Sambuca di Sicilia: wines from Sambuca in Agrigento.

Santa Margherita di Belice: wines from the Belice Valley. Varietals must contain 85 per cent of the grape named.

Sclafani Bagno: a wide variety of wines from an inland area between Palermo and Caltanissetta.

Good wine producers to look out for include Abbazia Sant'Anastasia, Duca di Salaparuta, Planeta, Regaleali-Conte Tasca d'Almerita and Tenuta di Donnafugata.

MOSCATO & MALVASIA DELLE LIPARI

Sicily has some fine dessert wines in addition to Marsala. Moscato di Pantelleria is one from Italy's most remote DOC zone, the volcanic 'Island of Winds', Pantelleria, near the coast of Tunisia. They produce an intensely fragrant sweet wine made from Zibiddo (large Moscato) grapes grown on low-trained vines. The basic variety has 12.5 per cent alcohol; sweeter and richer versions contain 17.5 per cent.

Moscato Passito di Pantelleria is made from sun-dried grapes. Occasionally you might see Moscato di Noto from the southeast, but Moscato di Siracusa now appears to be extinct. Good producers include Nuova Agricoltura, Donnafugata, Salvatore Murana and D'Ancona.

The fragrant DOC Malvasia delle Lipari is made from a grape brought to the Aeolian Islands of Lipari and Salina by the Greeks. Malvasia delle Lipari Naturale is produced from grapes that are picked when they have already begun to dry and then further dried on cane mats in the sun. Sometimes you can also find a honeyed Malvasia delle Lipari Passito. Producers include Carlo Hauner and Cantine Colosi.

Colazione e spuntini

Coffee in Palermo

Midsummer morning, and the blinding heat of the day already dances around the edge of your senses. The sounds of daily life jangle through the blistered streets, palm-filled piazzas and labyrinthine markets. You need a coffee. The short, sharp shock that jolts the nerve endings into a state of red alert from the mainline combo of rich arabica cut with astringent robusta beans preferred by all southern Italians. The cafés, already hazy with slate blue smoke, are filled with men, brooding, heavy-lidded and distantly flirtatious; they come for *ristretto*, a sweet roll or pastry, perhaps filled with ice cream, topped with a snowdrift of whipped cream or dipped into a lemon granita. At home, families keep a bottle of cold espresso in the fridge to sip throughout the day.

Distilled into miniscule cups, Sicilian coffee is high-octane, dark as midnight and syrupy-sweet, topped with the essential swirl of *crema*. You could tell fortunes from the grounds. Coffee consumption and attendant rituals are etched deep into the Latin soul. It is an essential punctuation to the daily routine, and the Sicilians understand the complex interaction of bean, blend, roast, grind and brew essential for the perfect mouthful. They appreciate coffee making is a precise technique, its drinking an art, and that roasting is the science that underpins the whole rite.

The Torrefazione Termini in Palermo has been roasting coffee for over 70 years, supplying the Bar Alba, acclaimed by *Gambero Rosso* magazine as serving the best coffee in Italy. The premises are unassuming: on one side, a marble service desk with grinding machine, hemmed in by bags of roasted, blended beans; on the other, for no apparent reason, a discount china counter.

The beans arrive raw, from all over the world, to be toasted in a drum roaster nearly as old as the shop, encrusted with pulleys and wheels and levers like the engine of a steam locomotive. As coffee roaster Giovanni Lo Verso explained, 'New roasters are shiny and impressive, but they don't give the same flavour. We roast the coffee the old way and it's still the best!'

All the time he talked, he was hovering around the roaster, adjusting the temperature, checking the colour of the beans (robusta and arabica, one of the house blends) and the amount of oil on the surface. 'Each bean has its own roasting time,' he said. 'It looks simple, but if you

'Drink it, drink it,' he urged. 'See – it explodes in your head like a bomb!' GIOVANNI LO VERSO

misjudge the length of roasting, even by seconds, then the coffee will taste like poison!' A convoluted Sicilian wave of the hand, then he continued: 'We can roast up to 250 kilos (550lb) at a time, but we just make what we need in order to sell it as fresh as possible. We start at 7am and continue roasting until about 3pm.'

A cascade of steaming mahogany-going-on-ebony beans erupted onto a cooling table, the paddles sweeping the hot beans around like a coffee windmill. Giovanni pointed out that all the beans were highly roasted. 'Any lighter and they simply don't taste good. I know you English, you drink coffee from beans that might as well be raw!'

We started talking about brewing coffee. My friend Rosy said you have to pack the coffee tightly in with a spoon, dampen it down really well, then take a toothpick and make several holes. Why? 'I don't know, that's the way we always make it. The important thing is it always works. And you need an old coffee pot, it makes coffee better than a new one. You never feel like throwing your old pot away.'

All this talk of espresso was giving everyone withdrawal symptoms. Giovanni organised thimbles of the black stuff an inch deep, promising strength without bitterness. 'Drink it, drink it,' he urged. 'See – it explodes in your head like a bomb!'

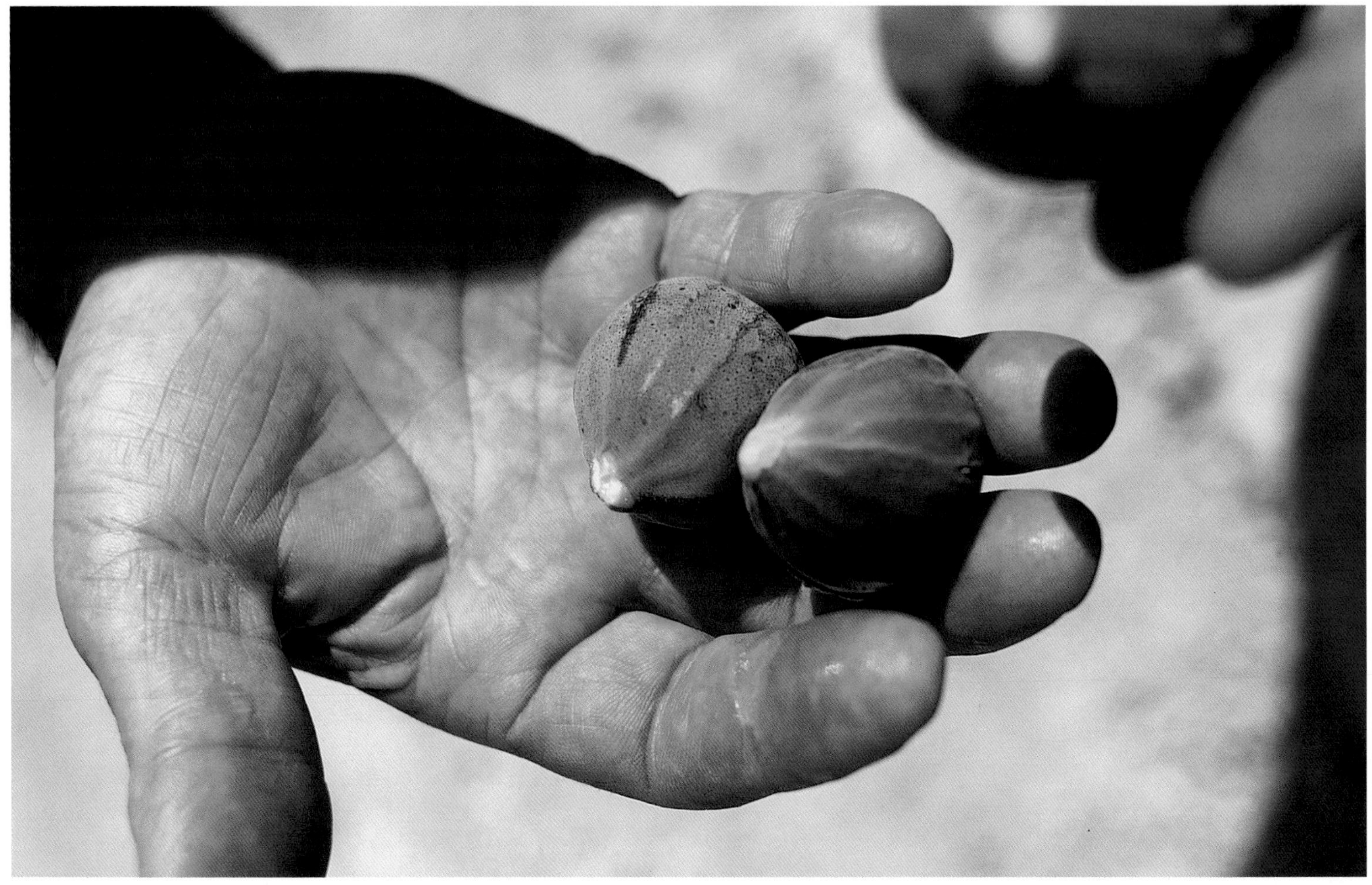

Aromatic baked figs

Figs and pomegranates: two ancient fruits, almost as old as time itself. Although figs grow wild in the Mediterranean, almost literally at the drop of a seed, they are also widely cultivated in Sicily. The best way to eat them is straight from the tree, warm from the summer sun, when a bead of golden nectar signals their fragile, squashy ripeness. Baking, however, brings out the flavour of necessarily immature imported fruit.

If figs are a symbol of sexuality, then fiery-coloured pomegranates represent fertility. They are considered the fruit of Persephone, the daughter of Demeter (goddess of agriculture), who was abducted by Hades from Lake Pergusa, near Enna. Persephone refused to eat until tempted by the pomegranate's translucent, crimson seeds. As a result, she was destined to spend half the year in the Underworld, returning to earth for the other half, bringing with her the renewal of spring.

Serves 3–4

12 fresh black figs
juice of 2 oranges
150ml/5 fl oz red wine
2 cloves
1 stick cinnamon
a little grated nutmeg
2 tbsp honey
pomegranate seeds or toasted almonds

Heat the oven to 180°C/350°F/Gas 4.

Cut the figs almost as if you were going to quarter them but stop short of the base. Place in an ovenproof dish.

Slowly heat the orange juice, red wine, cloves, cinnamon, a little nutmeg and the honey to taste (depending on how sweet the oranges are). Simmer for 5 minutes, then pour over the figs.

Bake in the oven for 10 minutes.

Serve at room temperature sprinkled with pomegranate seeds or toasted almonds.

'The orange blossom honey goes almost white; everyone thinks it's sugary, but it's just the way it was naturally meant to be.' CALOGERO AIELLO

Blood orange marmalade

The ancient fief of San Giuliano, situated between Catania and Syracuse, has belonged to the Marchesi di San Giuliano for 800 years. The exquisite San Giuliano preserves come from family recipes found in the personal cookbook of Maria, Duchess of Carcaci, grandmother of the present Marchese. They were made purely for family consumption until their commercial debut ten years ago, largely thanks to the entrepreneurial spirit of Fiamma di San Giuliano Ferragamo – a name more associated with elegant footwear than sticky fingers.

The business is now run by Fiamma's daughters, Giulia and Maria, who ensure that only the freshest, hand-picked, organic San Giuliano citrus fruit is used. The preserves are hand-made in small batches during the winter months, and the high percentage of fruit gives each crested jar its exceptional colour and quality. They suggest eating the preserves on toast, over ice cream, between layers of cake, on cheesecake, or simply by the spoonful.

This traditional way of making preserves from *I Dolci Siciliani* by Maria Adele di Leo, is similar to the San Giuliano method.

Makes 1.4 litres/2½ pints
900g/2lb blood oranges
1.7 litres/3 pints water
900g/2lb sugar
peel of 1 lemon
½ tsp butter

Wash the oranges, and pierce each one with a fork in several places. Steep in water for 24 hours.
Drain the oranges, reserving the liquid, and cut each orange into tiny pieces, discarding the seeds. It doesn't matter if the flesh and skin fall apart.
Place the chopped oranges and reserved liquid in a preserving pan with the sugar and lemon peel. Bring to the boil, then turn the heat down as far as possible and cook very gently for an hour.
Leave the marmalade to stand for another 24 hours. Reheat and boil for 30–40 minutes, stirring from time to time to prevent the marmalade sticking. Lower the heat if it looks like it will boil over.
Stir well, adding the butter to disperse any scum. Leave to settle for 15 minutes, then pour into sterilised jars and seal tightly.

Three citrus salad with honey & pinenuts

Calogero Aiello, of La Bottega dell'Ape in Caltanissetta, is one of Italy's top beekeepers, producing honey derived from almond blossom, eucalyptus, chestnut, wild cardoons, medlars, *mille fiori* and the luscious orange blossom of Catania. Even in Roman times, Caltanissetta was renowned for its honey. As Calogero explained, 'It is low in humidity, which makes the honey very thick, and of course it is unfiltered with no additives at all. It has an unrivalled intensity, because nature here is richer than anywhere else.' This simple fruit salad makes the most of fine honey and is enhanced by toasted pine nuts.

Serves 2
1 white grapefruit
1 red or pink grapefruit
2 oranges
2 tbsp runny honey
50g/2oz pinenuts

Peel and segment the citrus fruit. Remove the membrane and cut the flesh into chunks – this is best done by hand over a bowl so as to catch the juice.
Mix in the honey and leave to chill for several hours or overnight.
Just before serving, toast the pinenuts and scatter over the top.

Pignoccata di Linda

Popular honeyed fritters, fashioned in the shape of the pine cones Jesus allegedly used as childhood toys, and traditionally served on vine leaves. This recipe comes from Linda Ruggiero, a wonderful cook, who lives in a 19th-century villa with a lush garden in the small seaside town of Terrasini, near Palermo. Although they can be made by hand, it's a lot easier if you use a food mixer.

Serves 4–6
3 eggs
3 tbsp sugar
4 tbsp vegetable oil
300–400g/10–14oz flour
2 heaped tbsp clear honey
chopped almonds and/or hundreds and thousands (optional)

Break the eggs into a mixing bowl. Whisk in the sugar, then the oil.
If using a food mixer, change the whisk attachment to the dough hook before proceeding.
Add several tablespoons of the flour and keep mixing, adding more flour until the mixture thickens.
Place the dough on a floured work surface – if it feels too moist, add a little more flour. You want a soft but dry dough. Lightly flour your hands and knead the dough well.
Break off a piece of the dough and roll it into a long, thin sausage shape, then cut into 1cm/½in pieces, rather like gnocchi.
Heat about 2.5cm/1in of oil in a frying pan; it should be hot, but not so hot you see the heat haze rise. Add the pieces of dough and fry till brown, stirring occasionally and keeping the oil on a medium-high heat. Don't crowd the pan. Drain on kitchen paper.
Melt the honey in a separate saucepan over a low heat, then add the fried dough pieces and mix well with a wooden spoon so they are covered in the molten honey.
Take the pan off the heat and remove the sticky little balls with a slotted spoon or spatula. While they are still hot, arrange in a pyramid on a serving plate.
Scatter with chopped almonds or hundreds and thousands, if wished. Leave to cool before serving.

Sfinci di Rosy

All Sicilians adore the puffy, deep-fried sweet fritters called *sfinci*. There are many different versions, some filled with custard cream or flavoured with vanilla, some simply drizzled in honey or rolled in sugar, using a variety of dough bases and a multitude of techniques. Others are made with sweet rice and there is even a rather arcane recipe cooked by Benedictine monks using mashed potatoes sweetened with honey for the feast of San Martino.

Choux pastry is always popular for *sfinci*, and this is a quick method of making them I learnt from my friend and travelling companion Rosy Bartolotta in Cinisi.

Makes about 24
750ml/25floz water
250ml/10floz milk
2 tsp sugar
2 tsp butter or margarine
500g/1lb 2oz flour
oil for deep-frying
salt
melted honey, crushed roasted almonds or icing sugar, to serve

Pour the water and milk into a saucepan, adding the sugar, butter or margarine and a pinch of salt. Heat until it almost reaches boiling point, being careful not to let the mixture boil.
Add the flour, stirring vigorously until well combined. Turn the hot paste onto a work surface and let it cool a little.
While the paste is still warm, oil your hands and roll the dough into a big, thick sausage. Divide it in two, then into thin sausages about 13–15cm/5–6in long.
Deep-fry the sfinci until you see little bumps appear on the pastry. Use a thin wooden stick or knitting needle to fish them out of the oil and drain on kitchen paper.
Drizzle with melted honey and sprinkle with crushed, roasted almonds, or just sprinkle with icing sugar. Eat quickly as the honey will make the sfinci go soggy if they stand around too long.

Sfinci di San Giuseppe

Beignets for San Giuseppe's (St Joseph's) Feast Day

San Giuseppe takes top billing in the complicated hierarchy of Sicilian saints. His feast day, 19 March, is a huge event in the communal and religious year, a time to visit friends and family, going from house to house, eating, eating and eating, with leftovers donated to charity. Among his many other roles, San Giuseppe is the patron saint of pastry cooks, so his feast day is also the time for everyone to enjoy these ricotta-stuffed *sfinci*.

Makes about 24

275ml/10floz water
125g/4oz butter
a pinch of salt
150g/5oz flour, sifted
4 eggs
1 litre/1¾ pints oil

FOR THE FILLING

500g/1lb2oz ricotta, or more if desired
100–125g/3–4oz caster sugar
1 tsp vanilla extract
3–4 tbsp candied citrus peel, chopped
4 tbsp chopped bitter chocolate or chocolate buttons
2–3 tbsp orange liqueur or orange flower water (optional)

Make the filling by sieving the ricotta into a bowl and then adding the other ingredients. Mix well and set aside.

To make the pastry, place the water in a saucepan over a low heat. Add the butter and salt, stir to dissolve, then raise the heat and bring the mixture to the boil.

Add the flour all in one go. Reduce the heat again and stir the pastry until it clings smoothly together and not to the sides of the pan. Transfer to a bowl to cool down.

Beat the eggs into the dough one at a time. Don't add the final egg if you think it's going to make the pastry so soft that it won't hold its shape when prodded with the spoon.

Heat the oil to 180°C/360°F. Working in small batches, use two tablespoons to drop a spoonful of the batter into the oil. The fritters, once the initial gush of frying bubbles dies down, will bob about merrily and turn themselves over to brown (help them along if they don't).

When the fritters are more brown than gold and nicely puffed up, remove with a slotted spoon and drain on kitchen paper.

Slit open and stuff with the ricotta cream. Eat immediately and don't worry about the ricotta oozing all over your fingers and chin.

'The fertile land provides almonds, pistachios and hazelnuts in abundance, human ingenuity the dazzling array of ornate biscuits and sculptured cakes.'

I dolci Siciliani

One look in the window of a Sicilian *pasticceria* shakes the foundations of the so-called Mediterranean Diet. The sweetness of the nuts and sugar, marzipan and ricotta cream seem to waft in the air. Arabic yearnings for comfits of almond and sugar, cinnamon and nutmeg marry with the flamboyant excess of Spanish Baroque. All the sweeps, swirls and curlicues of the noble *palazzi* and churches crumbling in the hot sun like dry pieces of *pan di Spagna*, are mirrored in the Sicilian devotion to all things sweet. The fertile land provides almonds, pistachios and hazelnuts in abundance, human ingenuity the dazzling array of ornate biscuits and sculptured cakes that reaches its apotheosis in the aptly named Triumph of Gluttony, which is a riotous indulgence of flavour, colour, fat and calories.

The Arabs left their mark with pastries such as *cassata*, *cannoli*, *torrone*, *nucatuli* (soft fig biscuits), *sfince*, marzipan, candied fruits, *cotognata* (quince paste) and *mostarda*, made from aromatic must. The craft was taken to even greater heights of refinement and fantasy by nuns in Sicily's numerous convents, taught by their Saracen maids, ladies of the harem who had taken refuge during the Norman invasion. Every order, rich or poor, had its own speciality; there was intense competition between nuns as to whose sweets were the lightest, the sweetest, the most complex. Recipes, outlets perhaps for frustrated creative and emotional urges, were jealously guarded, their custodians prepared to see them consigned to oblivion rather than passed into the hands of another.

Wealthier orders were able to use produce from the estates of landowning families. Sweets such as *dolce riposi di Erice* or *fedde* stuffed with blancmange (termed the Chancellor's Buttocks), were perhaps used to boost the image of a convent in the cut and thrust of ecclesiastical rivalries. The Convent of Santo Spirito in Agrigento is one of the last still to practise the trade, counting out earthly delights such as *cuscus dolce* and *bocconcini di dama* from behind its iron grille. In his memoirs, Fulco, Duke of Verdura, remembers ornate sweets from various convents arriving 'in trays lined with multi-coloured paper and covered with tinsel and little sugar balls dipped in silver and gold'.

When the state confiscated church lands in the late 1800s, however, production was drastically reduced. Commercial pastry shops sprung up in their place, their style and techniques influenced by the arrival of a number of Swiss patissiers who brought with them millefeuilles and custards for their coffee shops where ladies of fashion could meet and eat tempting little pastries in an intimate, and slightly risqué, atmosphere.

Sicilian pastries and sweets also trace their roots back to country traditions. Ingredients are always simple – there is even one sweet made purely from honey alone – but the most important ingredient, creativity, springs from the depths of the Sicilian soul.

Sweetmeats still mark the passage of the year and assume symbolic roles on all special occasions. At Easter, as well as *cassata* and *cassateddi*, there are *agneddu pasquali*, marzipan lambs stuffed with citron preserves, bearing halos and tiny banners, and hard-boiled eggs in pastry baskets topped with a cross. Every child receives Technicolor sugar figurines on All Souls' Day, and the shops sell *ossa di morto*, hard biscuits with lumps of dried meringue to simulate cartilage. And fig-filled *buccellato* is the ubiquitous Sicilian equivalent of Christmas cake. The roster for saints' days is unchanging: *sfinci* for San Giuseppe, *cuccia* (a pudding of boiled wheat) for Santa Lucia. *Biscotti di San Martino* are dunked into new Moscato wine (the good man also happens to be the patron saint of drunkards), and there are key-shaped biscuits for San Pietro.

Although *cassata* and *cannoli* are found throughout Sicily, and throughout the year, many confections are still tied to time and place. Every town will have its own speciality. *Mustazzoli* (almond biscuits with cloves and cinnamon) in Messina, *crispelle* (fried rice in honey) in Catania, *zuppa angelica* (a cold chocolate, lemon and sponge pudding) in Enna, sweet meat pastries in Modica, *sfogliata* (baked cheesecake) in Polizzi Generosa, *torrone* in Caltanissetta… the list is as long as a Sicilian vendetta.

Even in sugary mouthfuls, there are questions of life and death. Candied fruits are embalmed in sugar, while *minni di virgini*, virgin's breasts, are taken a step further by the Catanians who recall Santa Agata, their patron saint, with little cakes iced like white marble with a strategic cherry on top; martyred by having her breasts cut off, she still carries them round on a plate in the city's churches to this day. Sicilians, with their intense emotional inner life and love of melodramatic gesture, reason that if you eat the body of Christ in Communion, why not the breasts of a saint? Another sickly-sweet reference to poor Agata are green marzipan olives, to commemorate the moment when she stooped to tie her shoelace and a wild olive tree flowered on the spot.

It is in marzipan modelling or *pasta reale*, however, that Sicilian extravagance and painstaking craftsmanship reaches a climax. In Palermo, almond paste replicas are still described as *frutta di Martorana*, after the convent where the nuns once hung marzipan oranges on the trees to play a gentle prank on a visiting archbishop. The Catanians particularly pride themselves on the art. At Savia, a pasticceria opposite the Bellini Gardens in Catania, there are baskets piled high with marzipan produce, as if from some paradisical hot-house – majestic strawberries, knobbly red tomatoes with a spidery green calyx, half-peeled mandarins and blue-green figs oozing honey. Then there are detailed replicas of seafood, spaghetti or fried eggs. Even the vase of red roses may turn out to be almond. Intense sweetness in a life of extreme bitterness: a very Sicilian theme.

'Brutti ma buoni' di Giovanna Cavasino

Erice's reputation for *dolci* comes from the elegant pastries once baked at the Convent of San Carlo. Competition is fierce, each bakery boasting recipes 'personally' given them by the nuns. At Il Tulipano, an attractive shop packed with alluring sweet and savoury confections, Giovanna Cavasino, a bespectacled dynamo with a diva's temperament, holds sway. Why was the shop named after a flower, I asked? 'My husband liked the name,' she shrugged impatiently, 'but don't write about him. He just sits downstairs and takes the money. I'm the hard-working one! And you can write that my *cassatelle* are incomparable, the best in Sicily!'

This last salvo was delivered with typical Sicilian hyperbole, but indeed they were. The pastry is made to her Marsalan grandmother's recipe with white wine, then stuffed with ricotta cheese, chocolate and citrus zest, deep-fried and dusted with icing sugar.

Giovanna's forcefulness belies the delicate touch of her industrious hands; her iced marzipan *dolci ericini* are perfect mouthfuls. These 'ugly but good' almond biscuits are her version of a popular nut biscuit found in various guises throughout Italy.

Makes 24
4 egg whites
a pinch of salt
125g/4oz ground almonds
125g/4oz sugar
zest of 2 lemons
2 tbsp honey

Heat the oven to 180°C/350°F/Gas 4 and line a baking sheet with greaseproof paper. Meanwhile, lightly whisk the egg whites with a pinch of salt.
Mix the ground almonds with the sugar and lemon zest. Add just enough of the whisked egg whites to achieve a soft paste, then stir in the honey.
Use two tablespoons to heap small mounds of the mixture onto the baking sheet. If the mixture is too thick, add more egg white; if too sloppy, add more ground almonds. Keep them well spaced.
Bake for about 15 minutes until the biscuits are golden-brown, then cool on a wire rack.

Biscotti 'i pan di Spagna'

Adapted from *Papa Andrea's Sicilian Table*, an evocative account by actor and food writer Vincent Schiavelli of the secrets he learnt from his Sicilian *monzù* grandfather. *Pan di Spagna* is an airy-light sponge cake made without fat and is the basis of many Sicilian cakes and desserts. *Biscotti* simply means twice-cooked.

Makes 36
225g/8oz flour
2 tsp baking powder
pinch of salt
200g/7oz sugar
100g/3½oz butter
4 eggs
150ml/5fl oz anisetta or Pernod

Heat the oven to 160°C/325°F/Gas 3. Grease and flour a baking tin measuring 30 x 23cm/12 x 9in.
Sift together the flour, baking powder and salt.
Cream the sugar and butter in a separate bowl, then mix the eggs in one at a time, followed by the anisetta.
Add the flour to the sugar, butter and eggs, mixing well to give a heavy batter. Place in the prepared baking tin.
Bake for 20 minutes until the cake is golden brown and dry inside when pierced with a toothpick or skewer. Leave the oven on.
While still in the pan, cut the sponge cake into strips 1cm/½in thick. Cut the longer strips into two or three sections.
Gently remove from the pan and place flat on a wire rack.
Place the rack of sponge slices in the oven (so they toast on both sides) until golden brown, about 20–25 minutes.

Coffee & almond biscuits

Makes about 20
- butter
- breadcrumbs
- 3 egg whites
- a pinch of salt
- 250g/9oz sugar
- 100ml/4floz water
- 250g/9oz ground almonds
- 3 tsp finely ground coffee
- vanilla icing sugar

Heat the oven to 150°C/300°F/Gas 2. Meanwhile, butter a baking tin measuring 30 x 18cm/12 x 7in and sprinkle with breadcrumbs.
Stiffly beat the egg whites with the salt. In a separate bowl, dissolve the sugar in the water, then add the almonds, coffee and whisked egg whites.
Pour the mixture into the prepared tin and bake for 50 minutes.
Cool in the tin, then cut into squares and dust with vanilla sugar.

Chitellini

An almond biscuit that unusually can be eaten hot or cold.

Makes 18
- 125g/4oz butter, softened
- 50g/2oz sugar
- 175g/6oz flour, sifted
- 50g/2oz almonds, finely chopped
- 1–2 tbsp water
- vanilla icing sugar

Heat the oven to 190°C/375°F/Gas 5.
Cream the butter with the sugar, then add the flour and chopped almonds. Sprinkle in just enough water so the pastry starts to cling together.
Use your hands (it helps to grease them with vegetable oil) to form the dough into chubby, little 'fingers' about 5cm/2in long.
Arrange on a greased baking sheet and bake for 20–25 minutes until light brown.
Dredge with vanilla icing sugar before serving.

Giovanna Colletto's chocolate tartufi

Makes about 24
- 250g/9oz plain biscuits, finely crushed
- 25g/1oz unsweetened cocoa
- 2 eggs*
- 125g/4oz sugar
- 75g/3oz butter, melted
- a few drops of vanilla essence
- 2 tbsp rum, or other liqueur
- finely chopped hazelnuts, almonds, cocoa or coconut, for coating

Mix the biscuits with the cocoa in a large bowl.
Beat the eggs with the sugar until creamy, then add the melted butter and vanilla essence.
Gradually blend the egg mixture with the biscuits. Blend in the rum and leave to firm up overnight.
Roll into balls and coat with nuts, cocoa or coconut, as wished.

***Note** that the biscuits and therefore the eggs, are uncooked. Avoid this recipe if in a vulnerable group.

Clockwise from far right: Chocolate Tartufi, Coffee and Almond Biscuits, Chitellini

Almonds & pistachios

The almond was brought to Sicily by the ancient Greeks, who already knew how to make a sort of marzipan with ground almonds and honey. The Arabs subsequently introduced sugar cane, and it was this inspired partnership that truly initiated the great tradition of Sicilian sweetmeats.

A sharp tongue is described in Sicilian dialect as *pizzuta*. The term also refers to the famous sweet almond grown around Avola near the golden Baroque city of Noto, and the name derives from the glorious shape of the shell that curvaceously sweeps round but ends in a spiky point. The exceptionally hard shell protects the nut from the sun and allows it to be stored longer, as if in compensation for the low yield from the tree.

These nuts melt in the mouth like ready-made marzipan, soft and rich, full of sweet oil. Their large, flat shape and consistent size (Sicilians are very particular about this) makes them suitable for sugared almonds: white for weddings; green for engagements; red for a degree; silver for a 25th anniversary; golden for a 50th wedding anniversary; pink and blue for births.

The almond tree flowers early here, and by the end of January the fields are already covered with scented blossom, like leftover snow. The almonds are picked in late summer, when the flavour is at its most intense. The fruit is shaken down with long poles, tumbling onto canvas sheets placed under the trees. After the husks are removed, they are dried in the sun before being cracked and hand-separated from the nuts inside.

Although much prized by top European bakers, Sicilian almonds are threatened by cheaper, overseas competition. 'In California, cultivation is more mechanised and less labour intensive,' explained Attilio Pagliarello, whose family have been almond merchants in Noto since 1923, 'but their almonds, compared to ours, taste dry and woody.' His elderly father stood silently to one side, watching every detail of the processing with eyes in the back of his head.

It was a similar story at Bronte, on the slopes of Etna. Unlike the muscular beauty of Catania, the black volcanic stone of the buildings here looked drab and unwelcoming, at least on a wet winter's day when the town seemed totally abandoned. But the satanic rock, dark earth and graveyard of tangled, skeletal trees concealed something of great beauty, a treasure trove of emerald pistachios. Pistachios that are a gift from God – with a little help from Signor Antonino Caudullo.

Every April, the impossibly contorted, ash-grey trees are resurrected with masses of yellow-green blossom presaging the new, oval leaves. 'They look like butterflies on the branches. It's a miracle that each year

such beautiful life comes from the bones of dead trees,' Signor Caudullo described with quiet devotion. By September the trees have a flushed look from the bunches of rose-pink husks that enclose the ivory-coloured shell and kernel – the prized nut itself, luminescent green, inside and out, streaked with amethyst and with an angelic, fragrant taste, but one that struggles also in the face of coarser, cut-price competition.

Initially taciturn and dubious of my motives, Signor Caudullo eventually began to relax and open up, telling me he had recently been honoured as a cavaliere by the Italian government in recognition of his life-long work with pistachios. He explained that the trees grow on rocky terraces and thorny ravines, making them virtually impossible to harvest mechanically. At harvest time, all the town turns out to pick them. It's backbreaking work, but as Signor Caudullo says: 'The more difficult the ground, the better the plant grows. Sometimes you even see a tree growing out of a cleft in the rocks.'

An ancient symbol of happiness, pistachios too arrived in Sicily with the Arabs. Bronte proved to be a perfect habitat, a marriage made in heaven between earth and plant. Today, Sicilian *pasticceria* would seem drab and monochromatic without the vivacious colour of pistachios, like a feast day without its saint.

Sicilian orange cake

This cake is adapted from *Agrumi*, a book on Sicilian citrus cooking by the distinguished Catanian food writer, Eleonora Consoli.

SERVES 6

FOR THE CAKE

2 eggs, separated
a pinch of salt
125g/4oz caster sugar
125g/4oz flour, sifted, plus extra for dusting
40g/1oz butter, melted, plus extra for greasing
grated zest of 2 oranges
1 tsp baking powder

FOR THE SYRUP

4 tsp sugar
juice of 1 orange

FOR THE ICING

juice of 1 orange
225g/8oz icing sugar
orange slices, orange leaves and/or silver sugared almonds, for decoration

Heat the oven to 180°C/350°F/Gas 4. Butter and flour a cake tin.
Whisk the egg whites with the salt until they form stiff peaks.
In a separate bowl, whisk the egg yolks and sugar until creamy.
Add the sifted flour gradually until the mixture resembles breadcrumbs. Mix in the melted butter, zest and baking powder.
Fold in the egg whites a little at a time. The mixture should be like a soft, sticky batter. Pour it into the cake tin.
Bake for 40 minutes or until the cake is dry when pierced with a skewer. Leave to cool until it is just warm to the touch.
Meanwhile, to make the syrup, dissolve the sugar in the orange juice over a low heat, then bring to the boil for 2–3 minutes. Remove from the heat and set aside.
Place the cake on a serving dish and make holes in the top with a skewer. Drizzle it with syrup, allowing the cake to absorb the liquid before adding any more. You may not need all the syrup.
Make the icing by mixing the orange juice with the icing sugar.
Spread it over the cake and, as it starts to dry, decorate with orange slices and leaves, and/or some sugared almonds.

Mazaresi

Little pistachio cakes

Mazara del Vallo, where these cakes originate, is a large fishing port with a wonderful collection of little-known Baroque monuments. It was the first town conquered by the Arabs in 827 and was once home to four peoples: Arabs, Jews, 'Latins' and Greeks, each with their own quarter. There is still a sizeable Tunisian population in the town living in the warren of arched alleys called the *kasbah*.

MAKES 24

200g/7oz shelled pistachios
salt
4 eggs, separated, plus 2 egg yolks extra
150g/5oz caster sugar
50g/2oz potato flour
grated rind of 1 orange
butter
icing sugar

Heat the oven to 160°C/325°F/Gas 4. Meanwhile, bring a pan of water to the boil and blanch the pistachios for 1 minute.
Drain the nuts then roll them dry in a clean tea-towel – this may help remove some of the fine papery skin around the nut, though it makes a mess of the towel.
Pound the nuts with a pinch of salt using a mortar and pestle, or grind them in a food processor.
Beat the egg whites with a pinch of salt until they form soft peaks.
In a separate bowl, mix the egg yolks and sugar, then stir in the potato flour, grated orange rind and pistachio paste.
Fold in the egg whites.
Butter some muffin or fairy cake moulds, or line them with cup-cake papers, and fill them two-thirds full with the cake mixture.
Bake for 30 minutes. Remove from the moulds and, when cool, dust with icing sugar before serving.

'If you want to live a long life, eat a little at a time.' SICILIAN PROVERB

Mazaresi (right)

Buccellato

Christmas ring

This rich Christmas sweet-pastry cake comes in many shapes, sizes and variations, with just as many recipes for the fruit and nut filling. Sun-dried figs are the one constant, although as Vincent Schiavelli wryly comments in *Papa Andrea's Sicilian Table*, figs were once only for the poor, the rich used raisins. Figs grow in abundance in Sicily, but the vines needed for raisins were scarce.

Makes 1 large cake

FILLING

125g/4½oz ready-to-eat dried figs
50g/2oz raisins
50g/2oz currants
150ml/5floz Marsala or rum
juice and zest of 1 orange
1 tsp cinnamon
a little grated nutmeg
200ml/7floz orange blossom honey
50g/2oz almonds, chopped
100g/4oz walnuts, chopped
50g/2oz bitter chocolate, grated

PASTRY

400g/14oz flour
150g/5oz icing sugar
175g/6oz butter, cubed
3 egg yolks, plus 1 egg white
grated zest of 1 lemon
a pinch of salt

TO FINISH

2 whole eggs, beaten
chopped pistachio nuts
candied fruit

To make the filling, finely chop the figs, raisins and currants or whizz them briefly in a food processor. Add the Marsala or rum, orange juice and zest, cinnamon and nutmeg and leave overnight.
Next day, place the mixture in a saucepan, add the honey and simmer over a low heat until sticky and toffee-like.
Mix in the almonds and walnuts and leave to cool. Then add the grated chocolate and set aside.
To make the pastry, sift the flour into a bowl and stir in the sugar.
Make a well in the centre and add the butter, egg yolks, lemon zest and salt. Work together with your fingertips to make a soft dough, then knead until it forms a soft ball.
Place the pastry on a baking sheet lined with silicone paper and roll into a log about 45cm/18in long. Cover and chill for 1–2 hours.
Flatten the chilled pastry log slightly and spoon the filling along the centre, leaving a gap of at least 1cm/½in on either side.
Beat the egg white and use it to moisten the edges of the pastry.

Fold the pastry over, pressing the sides together so that they form a long sausage shape. Using a knife, make several diagonal slashes on the top of the pastry.
Ease the ends of the sausage round to join together in a circle. Alternatively, curl into a horseshoe shape or leave as a log.
Glaze the pastry with some of the beaten egg, then chill for 30 minutes. Meanwhile, heat the oven to 160°C/325°F/Gas 3.
Bake for 20–25 minutes until puffed and golden.
Remove from the oven and brush with more of the beaten egg.
Press the chopped pistachios and candied fruit over the surface and return to the oven for a few minutes. Serve hot or cold.

Variation

For buccellatini, roll the dough into a sheet 0.5cm/¼in thick and cut into small circles with a pastry cutter. Moisten the edges with beaten egg white, then put some filling in the middle of each circle.
Fold over to form half-moons, brush with beaten egg and place 5cm/2in apart on a greased baking tray. Bake for 25–30 minutes at 160°C/325°F/Gas 3, then cool on a wire rack.
Alternatively, pinch off a piece of pastry about the size of a walnut, roll it into a ball, then flatten into a circle.
Spoon a little of the filling into the centre. Wrap the pastry over the fruit mixture, enclosing it completely, and roll into a ball.
Repeat with the remaining pastry and filling.
Place the balls at least 2.5cm/1in apart on a buttered baking tray and bake for 25–30 minutes at 160°C/325°F/Gas 3.
Remove to a wire rack to cool, then dust the little pastries with icing sugar before serving.

Frozen assets

'We stay in the royal palace and eat servings of ice cream as big as beefsteaks.'

Competition is fierce in the world of Sicilian ice cream. Twenty, thirty flavours, more – each *artigiano* enthusiastically going for the golden *gelato* with a palette of flavours from the traditional to the original, or downright bizarre. Every fruit in the book is iced and creamed, intently consumed in a cone or inside a sweet brioche. Novelty seekers are offered tiramisù, Ferrero Rocher, rum *croccantino*, tomato (one lick is enough), or a homage to Bart Simpson made with breakfast cereals. One famous *gelateria* in Bagheria even sells black, squid-ink ice cream. But the best flavours remain the old ones: black mulberry, almond, rose, cinnamon and pistachio. Jasmine blossom is the most exquisite of all.

The Sicilian passion for ice cream, sorbet and *granita* dates back to the Arabs who cooled their sweet fruit drinks with the snows of Etna, just as before them the ancient Greeks and Romans had once cooled their wine and mixed their fruit with snow. The next steps in this chilly history remains as opaque as a glass of almond milk; just how, when and where the technique of artificial freezing developed in the 17th century remains unclear, although the Sicilian Procopio Coltelli certainly played a part in the story at his legendary Paris café, Le Procope.

Snow, perhaps, seems a curious commodity for an island of such scorching summers, but it could be stored throughout the year in mountain caves then transported between insulating layers of salt and straw. It was the main source of income for the Bishop of Catania, a consecration perhaps of a celestial refreshment, as well as an example of astute, clerical moneymaking. Snow was a valuable export and ices a national obsession. A 19th-century follower of Garibaldi, writing from recently liberated Palermo, recorded: 'We stay in the royal palace and eat servings of ice cream as big as beefsteaks.' It is the transformation of the basic ice cream into the extravagant range of ornate bombes and cakes, however, that elevates a modest cone into Elizabeth David's 'jewellery of the table'. The catalogue makes tempting reading.

Spongato, for example, used to mean a sponge and ice cream cake, although now refers to a special sort of semi-soft ice. *Pezzi duri*, which date back to the 18th century, are layers of moulded ices, sliced into 'hard pieces'. Acireale in Catania is the birthplace of *spumone*, an ice cream bombe moulded around whipped cream; *schiumoni*, a variation on the theme, filled with frozen *zabaglione* or *semifreddo*. *Giardinetto*, a block of tri-colour ice cream and a rarity these days, is said to have been invented in honour of Garibaldi. And, above all, there is *cassata gelata*, baroque layers of vanilla and pistachio ice cream and rum-soaked sponge, studded with candied fruit and almonds and moulded around a filling of frozen Chantilly cream. *Exultate*!

254

Stella
LATTE INTERO
STERILIZZATO
A LUNGA CONSERVAZIONE

Antica

Strawberry ice cream

Serves 4–6

750g/1lb 10oz ripe strawberries, hulled

200g/7oz sugar

2 tbsp lemon juice

300ml/10floz double cream

Roughly mash the strawberries, sprinkle with the sugar and lemon juice, then leave to stand for a few hours.

Purée or blend the mixture well – if you don't like the minuscule strawberry seeds, press through a nylon sieve – and fold thoroughly into the double cream.

Churn in an ice cream maker until frozen.

Serve the ice cream as is, or use it in typically Sicilian style to fill a brioche, perhaps with the melon ice cream (right).

Melon ice cream

Serves 4–6

2 ripe, perfumed melons

120g/4oz sugar

juice of 1 lemon

400ml/14floz double cream

Cognac, for serving (optional)

Cut the melon into segments, then discard the seeds and cut away the flesh from the skin. Cut into chunks and sprinkle with sugar and lemon juice. Leave to stand for an hour.

Purée the mixture thoroughly.

Heat the cream gently (do not let it boil), then stir it into the purée.

Leave the mixture to cool, then chill it in the fridge for an hour or two before churning in an ice cream machine.

Serve the ice cream drizzled with Cognac, or plain in a brioche.

Chestnut & chocolate ice cream

Traditionally, many Sicilian ice creams are made with a cornflour base, *crema rinforzata*, without the use of cream or eggs at all. The method works best with non-fruit concoctions such as nuts or chocolate, both of which feature in this recipe.

Serves 4–6
1.2 litres/2 pints full-fat milk
225g/8oz caster sugar
2 heaped tbsp cornflour
100g/4oz plain, dark chocolate
435g/15oz unsweetened chestnut purée

Pour half the milk into a large saucepan, and stir in the sugar and cornflour until dissolved. Add the rest of the milk.
Place over a moderate heat. Carefully bring the mixture just up to boiling point, stirring constantly, and remove when the milk starts to make a lacy pattern around the edge of the pan. Act quickly as it should not actually boil. Set aside to cool.
Melt the chocolate and stir it into the cooled milk mixture along with the chestnut purée. Beat or blend well.
Chill for several hours before churning in an ice cream machine.

Cinnamon sorbet

Serves 4–6
3 sticks cinnamon
500ml/18fl oz water
150g/5oz sugar
50ml/2floz Martini Bianco

Infuse the cinnamon sticks in the water overnight, no longer.
Next day, bring to the boil, then remove from the heat.
Add the sugar and Martini and stir to dissolve, then discard the cinnamon sticks and leave to cool.
Churn in an ice cream machine until frozen.

Strawberry and melon ice creams in brioche (left), Coffee granita (right)

Coffee granita

Granita is a crunchy frozen slush – half-ice, half-drink – with a granular texture that is ravishingly refreshing on the sultriest of summer days. This one is coffee flavoured; a dollop of lemon *granita* is equally restorative, especially in a glass of iced tea.

Serves 4–6
125g/4oz sugar
125ml/4floz freshly made, strong espresso
350ml/12floz water
1 tbsp anisetta or sambuca
whipped, sweetened cream, to serve

Dissolve the sugar in the hot coffee, combine with the water and anisetta or sambuca. Leave to cool.
Pour into a shallow metal or plastic container, or ice cube trays, and freeze for 30–40 minutes.
When the edges of the granita have started to firm up but the centre is still liquidy, stir the mixture to break up the crystals.
Return to the freezer for another 20 minutes or so.
Stir again and place in the freezer. Repeat about every 20 minutes for the next few hours or until the granita has a set texture.
Serve immediately topped with whipped sweetened cream, or transfer to a covered plastic container to store and remove from the freezer about 30 minutes before serving.

SAIVATORE

Pranzo

Sicilian fish markets

Sicily is surrounded by three seas, with the catch varying between the seasons and between the trinity of different waters. A floor mosaic in the Roman Villa in the town of Piazza Armerina shows the local waters bursting with fish, simply there for the taking. Such enormous variety of fish makes the markets pulse with life.

Trapani is one of the loveliest, a semicircular Baroque square with grizzled, weather-beaten fishermen chewing on butt ends, shouting, joshing, cajoling you to buy. The fish are laid out in perfect geometric formations: little mackerel ready filleted, opened and flattened for frying; mottled chestnut and mustard moray eel; red and thorny scorpion fish; and calamari, narrow and conical alongside the cheaper, squatter *seppie* (cuttlefish). There are dripping string bags of *vongole veraci*, and other clams so fresh they squirt out water at anyone peering too inquisitively at their shells. In the midst of all the noisy vulgarity and barter, a fountain of a nymph, genteely déshabillé, adds a quiet note of unexpected grace.

Scenes from Catania fish market and Marinella

On the other side of the island, in Catania, a tough working city where feisty *nonne* weave through lawless traffic with one hand on the horn, the piazzas are chequered with an impenetrable brotherhood of men standing, talking, waiting, watching. The entrance to the frantic and colourful fish market is marked by a sheet of water that falls from the Fontana dell'Amenano, reputedly the waters of a mysterious river that flows through the city. The stallholders, more relaxed than in the western part of the island, let you nibble on raw anchovies or sea urchins as they describe the physical attractions of vast slabs of swordfish or tiny, transparent *nunnata* with all the enthusiasm of men in love with a piece of fish. All the buying is still done by men, a job, they unrepentantly assert, that is simply too important to be left to women.

Sicily has long taken its abundant source of fish for granted. However, in more recent times, as stocks have become increasingly depleted, fishing in the Sicilian seas has turned into open season in the Wild West. Short-term, individual need and greed versus conservation, social good and the rule of law; the dynamics of Sicilian society.

The best swordfish, sweet and juicy, are still caught in the mating season between April and June, when the fish swarm through the narrow, swirling currents of the Straits of Messina. Fishing in the mythical lair of Scylla and Charybdis is a dangerous and dramatic business; an 18th-century traveller described it as 'whale fishing in miniature'. The superstitious fishermen would recite an ancient Greek incantation to lure the fish closer to the boats, but, according to legend, if the great silver fish heard a word of Italian, they would slice beneath the waves like a dagger through a velvet curtain.

The tiny, black boats, traditionally fish-shaped in the belief this fooled the fish, have given way to vast fleets of feluccas with long thin prows and high masts; as stocks diminish, there is an increasing, illegal use of drift nets.

Swordfish has never been a fish for everyday eating; the catch is limited and commands a high price. The Messinesi are expert at cooking it. Two of the most popular methods are *alla ghiotta*, meaning appetising, with tomato sauce, celery, green olives and capers; and *involtini di pescespada*, skewers of thinly sliced fish wrapped around a filling of capers, tomatoes and olives. A courtly Messinese pie, made with orange-scented pastry, is filled with diced fish, tomatoes, celery, olives, capers, pine nuts and sultanas.

Tuna stocks, too, are fast disappearing, despite the fact that the earliest evidence of tuna hunting goes back to the 4,000-year-old cave painting of a bluefin on the tiny island of Lévanzo in the Egadi Islands. The catch was once huge; barrels of salted tuna along with ships' biscuits made from Sicilian wheat were essential shipboard provisions. Sicilian tuna, *Thunnus thynnus*, was much praised by Archestratus, and the Greeks even had a word that meant 'to watch for tuna'. In the Museo Mandralisca in Cefalù, there is a fine terracotta and black Greek *krater*, used to mix wine with water. The bell-shaped pot depicts a belligerent 4th-century fishmonger, ankle deep in fish heads, energetically chopping up tuna while he argues about the price with a difficult, sour-faced customer. Some things never change...

There are hundreds of recipes for tuna, but sweet-sour sauces sharpened with vinegar are typical of Sicily's classical heritage. Sometimes it is cooked *a sfinciuni*, meaning with onions, anchovies and 'strattu, or stewed with mint, garlic, cinnamon and cloves. In summer, it is frequently served cold with a *salsa verde* of capers, mint and anchovies or marinated with sweet-and-sour onions. A typically Syracusan flavouring is with potatoes, aubergines, peppers and tomatoes. If the tuna is really fresh, then it is best simply fried or grilled, sprinkled with a little lemon juice and dried wild oregano.

Sciacca, a working fishing port with a large Arab population, is famous for its spa and mud baths, praised by Pliny, and silvery anchovies packed crisscross fashion in barrels of salt, a practice little changed since the town was a Roman naval base. The Romans, in fact, used garum, fermented salted fish, to add a little zip to their cooking, much as the Sicilians use anchovies today.

Sicilian sardines are really young pilchards that swim in large shoals around the coast. Salted sardines were once twice the price of anchovies, but now that anchovy fishing is theoretically controlled by law to avoid damaging stocks, sardines are more abundant and cost less. The two most famous Sicilian sardine recipes are *pasta con le sarde* and *sarde a beccafico*, but sardines are often served simply fried. In fact an old proverb says that a good plate of fish should be fresh, fried and free – and cooked by someone else.

'If you want to eat fresh fish, you mustn't have a tight wallet.' SICILIAN PROVERB

Red mullet with saffron & herbs

Fried mullet is also often served with a pounded, sweet-and-sour sauce made with breadcrumbs, anchovies, parsley, mint, capers, sugar and vinegar.

For 4
flour
4 red mullet (weighing about 250g/9oz each)
4 tbsp olive oil
chopped herbs such as parsley, thyme, rosemary, fennel or dill
2 cloves garlic, chopped
1 onion, chopped
50ml/2fl oz dry white wine
2 tomatoes, peeled, seeded and chopped
1 tsp saffron strands, soaked in a little warm water
salt
peperoncino or black pepper
2 bay leaves
lemon quarters, for serving

Lightly dust the fish with flour. Heat the oil and fry quickly on both sides. If you haven't got a pan large enough to hold all the fish, use two pans, side by side.

Turn the heat down and strew a covering of herbs, garlic and onion over the fish. Pour in the wine, then add the tomatoes and saffron. Season to taste.

Top with the bay leaves, cover the pan and cook for a further 10 minutes. Serve with chunks of lemon.

Sea bass with lemon & black olives

Archestratus of Gela wrote the world's first gastronomic guidebook. The 4th-century Sicilian Greek with a razor-sharp palate and strong opinions describes in *The Life of Luxury* a journey around the Mediterranean in search of the best produce and the best cooking techniques. The fragments of the poem that remains emphasise freshness and quality; he writes mostly about fish and advises, in a very contemporary tone, that the best way to cook good fish is to 'simply sprinkle these lightly with salt and brush with oil for they possess in themselves the fullness of delight'. In other words, keep it simple.

For 2
1 large lemon
1 tbsp olive oil
dried oregano
salt
peperoncino or black pepper
4 fillets of sea bass, depending on size (allow 125–150g/4–5oz each)
black olives
fresh parsley, chopped

Squeeze half the lemon into a bowl, add the olive oil, a pinch of oregano, salt and peperoncino or black pepper and whisk vigorously or blend until emulsified.

Place the fish in an ovenproof dish and cover with the lemon marinade and the other half of the lemon, thinly sliced. Refrigerate for several hours.

When ready to cook, heat the oven to 180°C/350°F/Gas Mark 4. Remove the lemon slices from the fish and reserve. Bake the fish for 10 minutes, spooning over the marinade periodically. A few minutes before it's ready, throw in the black olives so they warm through and plump up nicely.

Decorate before serving with the reserved lemon slices and some chopped parsley.

Red mullet with saffron & herbs (left), The shore at Sarina (right)

Baked hake Palermo-style

There is a Sicilian saying that cynically points out that fish rots from the head down – a political or piscine observation?

For 2

1 whole hake, about 700–800g/1lb 10oz, scaled and gutted
salt
rosemary sprigs
olive oil
6 anchovies
peperoncino or black pepper
breadcrumbs
lemon quarters, for serving

Preheat the oven to 180°C/350°F/Gas Mark 4. Season the stomach cavity of the fish with salt and stuff with the rosemary sprigs dipped in olive oil.

In a small pan, gently melt the anchovies in a little oil and spike with peperoncino.

Arrange the fish in an oiled baking dish and pour over the anchovy sauce – push a little into the cavity of the fish as well. Sprinkle with breadcrumbs and drizzle with extra oil, if necessary.

Bake for 25–30 minutes and serve with chunks of fresh lemon.

Swordfish 'stemperata'

In the 4th century, Archestratus described the Sicilian practice of covering inferior fish with sauces 'rent with pungent vinegar'. Sweet-sour sauces are still popular in Sicily, the tartness of vinegar balanced by the 'sweet salt' introduced by the Moors. The word *stemperata* refers to the process by which the vinegar evaporates during cooking. Without the potatoes, this is also a popular sauce for serving with tuna.

For 4

500g/1lb 2oz waxy potatoes
2 large onions, finely chopped
olive oil
2 sticks celery, sliced
12 green olives, stoned and chopped
2 large tomatoes, peeled, deseeded and chopped
2 tbsp capers
4 tsp sugar
4 tbsp red wine vinegar
salt
4 swordfish steaks
flour
peperoncino or black pepper
fresh parsley, chopped

Preheat the oven to 180°C/350°F/Gas mark 4. Meanwhile, peel and boil the potatoes, then slice 1.5cm/½in thick and set aside.
Fry the onion in a little olive oil over a medium heat. When it starts to soften and colour round the edges, add the celery and olives. Cook for a few minutes more, then add the tomatoes.
Simmer for 5 minutes, occasionally stirring, then toss in the capers, sugar and red wine vinegar. Cook over a high heat to evaporate the vinegar – not too much as the celery should still have a crisp edge. Check the seasoning – the balance between sweetness and acidity is important – and set aside.
Salt the swordfish and dredge with flour. Fry in a little olive oil over a medium heat for 2 minutes on each side. Set aside.
Lightly oil an ovenproof dish, then cover the base with the slices of potato. Arrange the swordfish steaks on top and cover with the tomato sauce.
Bake for 10 minutes and serve sprinkled with chopped parsley.

Swordfish with mint & lemon (left)

Swordfish with mint & lemon

This recipe is an adaptation of one from cookery writer Diane Seed, who teaches cookery classes in Sicily and at her palazzo home in Rome.

For 4

25g/1oz fresh mint, chopped
100g/4oz capers, chopped
grated zest of 1 lemon
4 tbsp fresh lemon juice
6 tbsp olive oil
1 large clove garlic, finely chopped
1 tbsp chopped fresh parsley
4 swordfish steaks
salt
peperoncino or black pepper

Mix together the mint, capers, lemon zest, half each of the lemon juice and oil, plus the garlic, and some salt and peperoncino to make a salsa. Set aside.
In a shallow dish, combine the remaining oil and lemon juice, the parsley, some salt and peperoncino for a marinade.
Dip both sides of the swordfish in the marinade, then arrange the swordfish in the dish. Cover with plastic film and refrigerate for 1–2 hours, turning occasionally.
Grill for 3–4 minutes on each side. Alternatively, cook on a cast-iron, ridged pan. Serve topped with the mint salsa.

Swordfish alla ghiotta

For 4

50ml/2floz olive oil
1 onion, finely chopped
25g/1oz fresh parsley, chopped
1 stick celery, chopped
2 cloves garlic, finely chopped
150ml/5floz tomato sauce
1 tbsp capers
80g/3oz green olives, chopped
salt
peperoncino or black pepper
4 swordfish steaks
fresh basil leaves

Heat the oil in a large frying pan and sauté the onion until it wilts.
Add all the other ingredients except the fish and basil, stir well and simmer for 10 minutes.
Check the seasoning, then add the fish and spoon some of the sauce over it. Cover and cook on a low heat for 10 minutes.
Serve the fish and sauce sprinkled with torn basil leaves.

Tuna in tomato sauce with peas, Marsala & mint

For 2	400ml/14floz tomato sauce
2 tuna steaks	a handful of mint leaves, roughly chopped
olive oil	salt
1 large onion, finely sliced	50g/2oz petit pois
1 clove garlic, finely chopped	flour
peperoncino or black pepper	
1 tbsp Marsala	

Soak the tuna in cold water for 10 minutes, then rinse and pat dry.
Fry the onion in some olive oil until soft and lightly golden, then add the garlic and peperoncino.
As soon as you can scent the garlic, add the Marsala. Swish it round and let it bubble, then add the tomato sauce and most of the mint leaves. Check the seasoning and simmer for 10 minutes.
Add the peas, then cook gently for another 5 minutes.
In another pan, heat some olive oil. Lightly salt the tuna, coat in flour and shake off the excess. Fry over a medium-high heat for 1–2 minutes on each side.
Remove the tuna steaks with a slotted spoon and add to the pan containing the tomato sauce. Spoon a little of the sauce over the top of the steaks, cover and leave to cook over a low heat for 10 minutes. Serve sprinkled with the remaining mint leaves.
Any leftover sauce can be used for pasta the next day.

Sweet & sour tuna (above)

Sweet & sour tuna

For 4	125ml/4floz red wine vinegar
4 tuna steaks	2 tbsp sugar
salt	3 tbsp Marsala
flour	50g/2oz sultanas
3 tbsp extra-virgin olive oil	2–3 bay leaves
1 large mild onion, sliced	10 large green olives, stoned

Soak the tuna in cold water for 10 minutes. Rinse and dry. This helps to tenderise and lighten the colour.
Salt the fish, then dredge with flour, shaking off the excess. In a large frying pan, heat the olive oil over a medium heat.
Add the onion and sauté until translucent.
Push the onion slices to the edge of the pan. Add the tuna and cook, turning once, for about 3 minutes on each side.
Stir in the rest of the ingredients. Reduce the heat to low and simmer for 5 minutes to allow the flavours to blend.
Check the seasoning, then turn off the heat. Cover the pan, and allow the tuna to stand for 10 minutes to absorb the pan juices.
Discard the bay leaves before serving.

Marinated tuna with onions

For 4	250ml/9fl oz water
4 tuna steaks	1 tbsp sugar
salt	50ml/2floz vinegar
flour	25g/1oz fresh mint or parsley, chopped
olive oil	peperoncino or black pepper
2 large onions, thinly sliced	

Soak the tuna in cold water for 10 minutes. Rinse and dry.
Salt and lightly flour the tuna, then fry over medium-high heat in olive oil for 1–2 minutes on each side. Arrange on a serving dish.
Sauté the onions in the same oil, adding a drop more if necessary. When they start to colour, add the water and leave to simmer until the water has evaporated.
Dissolve the sugar in the vinegar and spritz it over the onions.
Bring to the boil, then reduce to a simmer. Stir in the chopped mint or parsley, salt and peperoncino and pour over the tuna.
Leave to cool, then refrigerate for several hours before serving.

Polpette di tonno di Rosa Ponzio

Rosa Ponzio cooks at Il Pescatore, her cousin's restaurant in the centre of Favignana Town. The white-walled restaurant is colourfully decorated with ceramics and paintings, photographs of the *mattanza*, fishing nets and the gaffs used by tuna fishermen. After spaghetti with tomato, wild herbs, capers, almonds and garlic, and a plate of *cicireddu*, deep-fried tiny fish like whitebait, she passed on this recipe for a fresh tuna dish made only during the fishing season. You can also poach the *polpette* in the sauce without frying first.

For 4

FOR THE POLPETTE (TUNA BALLS)

500g/1lb tuna
2 eggs
a handful of parsley, chopped
1 clove garlic, finely chopped
50g/2oz pine nuts
50g/2oz currants
100g/4oz breadcrumbs, plus extra for coating
100g/4oz Parmesan cheese, grated
zest of ½ lemon
2 tbsp chopped mint
salt
100ml/4floz olive oil

FOR THE SAUCE

2 sticks celery, chopped
2 tbsp chopped mint
a handful of parsley, chopped
2 cloves garlic, finely chopped
zest of ½ lemon
75g/3oz pine nuts
75g/3oz currants
a handful of basil, chopped
peperoncino
400g/14oz canned tomatoes
1 tsp 'strattu or 2 tsp tomato paste
1 tbsp lemon juice
1 tbsp brandy
200g/7oz tuna, finely diced

Soak the tuna for the sauce and the polpette in cold water for 10 minutes, then rinse and pat dry.

Finely chop the tuna for the polpette either with a knife or in a processor, ensuring it does not turn into a paste.

Mix the eggs, parsley, garlic, pine nuts, currants, breadcrumbs, cheese, lemon zest, mint and some salt into the tuna.

Shape the mixture into large balls and coat each one in some of the extra breadcrumbs, flattening lightly.

Heat the olive oil in a frying pan and brown the polpette on both sides. Set aside.

Add the celery, mint, parsley, garlic, basil and a little peperoncino (not too much or it will overwhelm the minty flavour) to the pan in which you cooked the polpette and sauté.

Add the canned tomatoes, their juice, the tomato concentrate, lemon juice and some salt and simmer for 5 minutes. Add the brandy and cook a few minutes longer.

Gently stir in the tuna chunks, covering them well with the sauce, and simmer for a further 5 minutes.

Lay the tuna balls over the sauce, overlapping if necessary. Moisten each one with a little sauce but do not submerge them.

Cover and simmer for 30 minutes. If the sauce seems very liquidy, take off the lid for the last 10 minutes – it should be quite thick.

Salt cod with oranges & olives

Baccalà, salt cod, is still a part of the traditional Christmas Eve meal in Sicily. This is a recipe from Trapani, adapted from *La Cucina Siciliana di Gangivecchio* by Wanda and Giovanna Tornabene. They have substituted the original juice of sour oranges with a mix of sweet orange and lemon juice.

For 4

1kg/2lb salt cod fillet, soaked in several changes of water for 24–48 hours
flour
olive oil
1 red onion, chopped
juice of 2 oranges
juice of ½ lemon
12 green olives, pitted and chopped
peperoncino or black pepper (optional)
orange slices, to garnish

Cut the fish into chunks and coat with flour. Sauté in olive oil, over a medium-high heat. Remove from the pan and set aside.
In another pan, heat a little olive oil and fry the onion until it wilts, then add the orange and lemon juices and the olives. Check the seasoning (you may not need any salt) and simmer for 5 minutes.
Add the fish, simmer for a further 5 minutes, then serve decorated with orange slices.

Salt cod in tomato sauce

Salt cod, stockfish and salted herring have been imported and eaten in Sicily since Norman times, when they were traded for wheat. It may seem curious that an island surrounded by an abundance of fresh fish should enjoy eating it preserved, but the reason is perhaps threefold: in past centuries, fresh fish was often too expensive; it could be eaten during the winter when the catch was poor and fishermen were unable to go out on the boats; and it was a source of protein for those living in the remote, mountainous interior far from the coast. There are many different recipes for salt cod in Sicily, but this one, cooked in a spicy tomato sauce, is universally popular.

For 4

1kg/2lb salt cod fillet, soaked in several changes of water for 24–48 hours
a few parsley sprigs
vinegar
2 large onions, chopped
400ml/14fl oz tomato sauce
200g/7oz black olives, stoned
2 tbsp capers
dried oregano
100g/4oz breadcrumbs
olive oil
salt
peperoncino or black pepper

Preheat the oven to 180°C/350°F/Gas Mark 4. Meanwhile, poach the salt cod in water with some parsley and a few drops of vinegar for 15 minutes.
Drain and let the fish cool. Skin and bone it, then separate the flesh into chunks and arrange in an oiled ovenproof dish.
Fry the onions in olive oil until they start to soften, add the tomato sauce and simmer for 20 minutes.
Throw in the black olives, capers and a little oregano and cook for a few minutes more. Season to taste.
Pour the tomato sauce over the fish, sprinkle with breadcrumbs, drizzle with oil and bake for 20–30 minutes.

Salt cod with oranges & olives

The salt of Trapani

There is an end-of-the-line feeling to Trapani, the last stop before Africa, yet this is where much of the story of Sicily begins. Greek mythology holds that the ancient, seafaring city, extending along a curving tongue of land, was founded where the Titan Cronos castrated his father Uranus, a Greek god who personified the sky, and threw his genitals into the sea.

Despite its modern urban sprawl, Trapani still boasts an eerily beautiful skyline and a Moorish and medieval town centre ringed with palm trees. DH Lawrence described it as a place still waiting for the Crusaders to call once more on their way to the East. It remains a port of importance, and is the home of the beautiful Madonna di Trapani, a statue credited with miraculous powers. At Easter, thousands come to watch the *Processione dei Misteri*, as groups of sculpted figures made by 17th-century guildsmen are paraded day and night in an increasing crescendo of fervour and emotion.

The Guild of Salt Makers must have been one of the wealthiest and most powerful of its day, when the glittering white salt pans and windmills stretched as far as the eye could see. 'Don Quixote would have gone off his head,' quipped Lawrence. It is a popular stopping place for migrating birds, who feed on the fish in the basins and lagoons.

The production of salt began here on the tiny island of Motya, once the site of a great Punic city. After the Phoenicians, it flourished in Roman times, like an ancient Royal Mint; the word 'salary' refers to the allowance given to legionnaires to pay for salt. At one time there were around 100 mills, enjoying great prosperity under the Spanish house of Aragon; the salt was even exported to Norway, where it was used to preserve dried cod. Now, only a handful of active windmills remain, the others stand like ghostly sentinels against the molten setting sun. Inside each mill an Archimedes' screw, powered by the force of the rotating vanes, controls the flow of water, and at one time the grinding of the salt as well.

The unrefined, mineral-rich crystals are prized for their sharp intensity of flavour, undiluted by estuarial water. The salt is produced by natural evaporation, a product of the wind and sun and sea. The lagoon provides perfect conditions – shallow, salty water; stifling heat so the salt dries quickly; strong, dry winds to turn the windmills' vanes. Collected during the summer months, the salt is left to dry out in piles over the winter like grubby snow drifts, protected by terracotta tiles to maximise the humidity.

The exhibition in the Museo del Sale in Nubia describes how workmen once carried buckets of salt weighing 30kg/66lb, cushioned by pillows on their shoulders. They wore belts with wooden pegs and holes to note the number of buckets filled. When they reached 24,000 buckets, they would sing a hymn of thanks to God for *il sale di Sicilia*.

Sarde a beccafico

Stuffed sardines

A speciality of Palermo, this recipe takes its name from the supposed resemblance to the *beccafico*, a plump little bird whose rump and tail feathers stick up in the air as it feeds on figs in the trees. Although it is a traditional Easter dish, these filleted sardines stuffed with breadcrumbs, currants, pine nuts and flavoured with bay leaves and citrus juice, are also served throughout the year, often as part of the restaurant antipasto table. Ingredients may variously include toasted almonds, parsley, capers or anchovies, but passions run high on the subject. For example, the use of mint in this recipe could be regarded as dangerously radical, but perhaps not something necessitating a horse's head on my doorstep. When served, the sardines look wonderful, a sort of racy Sicilian cousin to the old-fashioned British soused herring.

To make 24

24 fresh sardines
olive oil
½ onion, finely chopped
200g/7oz breadcrumbs
50g/2oz currants
50g/2oz pine nuts
fresh mint, chopped
juice of 1 orange
juice of ½ lemon
24 bay leaves
salt and pepper

Your fishmonger may prepare the sardines for you, although you might have to beg. If not, proceed as follows.

Wash the sardines and de-scale them as necessary.

Take a deep breath, and give yourself plenty of time. It's not hard, only fiddly. Break off the sardine heads with a twist and snap movement. With luck, most of the guts come away with the head, which makes the next step easier.

Slit open the belly of the fish and use your thumb and fingers to draw out the remaining innards. Cut off the fins, then lie the fish on its belly and press lightly but firmly on the spine – it should give way with a small plop and the fish will lie flat like an open book.

Turn the fish over and insert your thumb under the spine, about halfway along the body. Gently lift it up and use a thumb or finger to run under the rest of the spine, separating it from the flesh. Snap it loose where the spine bone meets the tail. You need to keep the tail on – this is the whole point of the name of the dish.

Rinse under running water, getting rid of any unpleasant bits or leftover fins – you can feel with your hands if there are any large bones left. In theory there shouldn't be, but that's theory for you.

Set aside while you make the filling. The worst part is over.

Preheat the oven to 180°C/350°F/Gas Mark 4.

Heat 2 tbsp of oil in a pan and sauté the onion until soft but not coloured. Add the breadcrumbs and keep stirring until the crumbs are toasted. Do not let them burn.

Take off the heat and stir in the currants, pine nuts, mint, and some salt and pepper. Moisten with half the orange and lemon juice plus a little olive oil. Carefully mix well together.

Drain off any excess liquid from the sardines, then lay them skin-side downwards.

Place a teaspoon of the stuffing on each one and roll up from the head end to the tail. Pack them tightly in an oiled baking dish, arranged with the tails pointing upwards; place a bay leaf between each sardine so they don't unroll.

Drizzle the sardines with the remaining orange and lemon juice, some salt and olive oil. Bake for 15 minutes. Serve cold. *Bravo!*

North African legacy

'At one time, they say, you could smell it in the air on Sunday mornings, regular as Mass, whisps of aromatic steam escaping from each kitchen's jealously guarded recipe.'

It may come as a surprise to find that one of the classic dishes of western Sicily is cuscus, but it is a tangible reminder that North Africa is closer to the island than Rome. *Cuscus* arrived in the culinary baggage of 11th-century Arab rulers; it is a legacy, also, of the small Sephardic Jewish communities that once flourished here until dispersed by the Spanish Inquisition. Trade with Tunisian merchants reinforced the habit, but although there are a few places where it is made with lamb, chickpeas and potatoes scented with cinnamon, fish is more customary, and its consumption is intertwined with ancient mystique, household ritual, dreams and desire.

At one time, they say, you could smell it in the air on Sunday mornings, regular as Mass, whisps of aromatic steam escaping from each kitchen's jealously guarded recipe. Trapanese women insist it takes much practice, strength and delicacy to make a good *cuscus* – far moister than its Maghreb cousins, steamed with a different method.

The correct ingredients include two grades of semolina made from the Sicilian wheat *grano duro*, and two categories of fish (for stock and for the table). Instructions are not just precise, they assume the status of culinary legislation. Only the right conical terracotta bowl in which to make and rest the *cuscus* will do; only the right *cuscusera* in which to steam the grain must be used, placed over just the right pot.

Each step, like stages of the Cross, has its own arcane terminology: from the pin-head pellets produced by rubbing in a rotary motion with one hand while sprinkling salted water over the grain with the other, to the flour and water paste used to seal the pans as they steam. When the *cuscus* is finished, it is tucked up in a woollen blanket like a child and set aside to rest, *si metti a dormiri*. It all serves to heighten the sense of anticipation for a dish that demands time, patience and peace of mind. Meditation may help. Hypnosis, possibly. Failing that, rest assured that even the Sicilians buy ready-prepared *cuscus* these days – even if they don't admit it.

A curiosity: *cuscus dolce* is a sweet speciality of the sisters of the 12th-century Monastero di Santo Spirito in Agrigento. It is made from semolina mixed with finely chopped almonds and pistachios and decorated with cinnamon, candied fruit and nuts, composed however in such a fashion as to deceive the eye into thinking it is the savoury original. A typical Sicilian trompe l'oeil.

Fish cuscus

The following (very simplified, practically deconstructed) recipe is based on one from San Vito Lo Capo, a popular beach resort with stunning beaches that holds an annual *cuscus* festival in September of *musica, mare e delizie* – music, seafood and delights.

For 6

FOR THE BROTH

1 onion, roughly chopped
4 cloves garlic
peperoncino
olive oil
1 tbsp 'strattu or 2 tbsp tomato paste
750ml/1 pint 7floz fish stock
750ml/1 pint 7floz water
50g/2oz almonds chopped
fresh parsley, chopped
1.5kg/3lb 5oz mixed fish, such as mullet, bass, bream, conger eel, John Dory, hake
steamed mussels and prawns, to garnish

FOR THE CUSCUS

500g/1lb 2oz pre-cooked couscous
2 large onions, finely chopped
olive oil
1 cinnamon stick
2–3 cloves
toasted almonds, flaked
fresh parsley, chopped
2–3 bay leaves
salt and black pepper

Preheat the oven to 150°C/300°F/Gas 2.

Cook the couscous according to the instructions on the packet. Meanwhile, fry the onions gently in a little oil until golden.

Mix the warm couscous with the onions, cinnamon stick, cloves, almonds, parsley, bay leaves, salt and black pepper. Drizzle with olive oil and place in a casserole dish. Cover tightly and place in the oven while you make the fish broth.

For the broth, brown the onion, garlic and peperoncino (the broth should be quite spicy) in a little oil in a large pan. Add the 'strattu and cook a little longer.

Pour in the fish stock and water and flavour with the almonds and parsley. Season well with salt. Bring to the boil, then turn the heat down and poach the fish gently for about 15 minutes.

Remove the fish with a slotted spoon. Skin and bone the fish and divide into small portions. Strain the liquid. Check the seasoning.

Fluff up the couscous and pour over two-thirds of the broth, so it becomes quite moist. Mix in the reserved pieces of fish, and sprinkle liberally with parsley.

Reheat the remaining broth and serve in a jug alongside. Garnish with the cooked mussels and prawns.

Taormina

Baked mussels

The best mussels in Sicily are said to come from the lakes of Ganzirri, a lively summer resort near Messina, where the brackish ponds, linked to the open sea by feeder channels, provide perfect conditions for farming mussels. This recipe is a version of one found throughout Sicily.

For 2 main courses or 4 starters

1.5kg/3lb mussels
150ml/5floz white wine
2 cloves garlic, peeled but left whole
olive oil
1 onion, finely chopped
6 anchovies, chopped
peperoncino or black pepper
50g/2oz capers
chopped parsley
150g/6oz breadcrumbs
juice of 1 lemon

Preheat the oven to 220°C/425°F/Gas Mark 7. Clean the mussels and place in a large covered pan with the wine and garlic. Cook for 5 minutes over a medium heat, shaking the pan as they steam. Discard any that do not open. Strain the juice and reserve.

As soon as they are cool enough to handle, snap off one shell from each mussel and place the mussels in a single layer in a large baking dish or on a baking sheet.

Fry the onion in olive oil until golden and soft. Reduce the heat and stir in the anchovies until they break up and melt.

Add the peperoncino, capers, parsley and breadcrumbs and stir so that all the breadcrumbs take on some flavouring. Moisten with extra olive oil, if necessary.

Aim to top each mussel with a spoonful of this mixture, but you are more likely to end up with blanket coverage over and around each one. It won't matter. Drizzle with olive oil and lemon juice and bake for 5 minutes.

Remove from the oven and sprinkle with the reserved cooking juice. Bake for a further 5 minutes, and serve straightaway.

'When you eat, close the door, and when you talk, make sure no one is listening.' SICILIAN PROVERB

Riso con gli angeli

Seafood rice 'with the angels'

Although rice was originally planted in Sicily by the Saracens, and was grown in Catania until the 18th century, there's still many a Sicilian who believes a meal is not a meal without pasta. An old saying warns that: 'Rice weighs you down but doesn't lift you up.' But attitudes are changing as risotto becomes more fashionable. It's popular, for example, to serve both pasta and rice dishes, such as champagne risotto, at weddings. There is no particular explanation for the name of this dish, other than it tastes divine. It is not a risotto, so you do not need to keep stirring it.

For 2

4 tbsp olive oil
4 cloves garlic, finely chopped
150g/5oz squid, cut into rings or pieces
150g/5oz prawns, shelled and de-veined
500g/1lb cooked mussels, removed from their shells, plus a few reserved shells
salt
peperoncino or black pepper
1 large, ripe tomato, skinned, deseeded and chopped
25g/1oz parsley, chopped
4 tbsp dry white wine
400g/14oz arborio rice
2 large pinches saffron strands, soaked in a little hot water

Heat the olive oil in a large pan or casserole and lightly sauté the garlic. Before it browns add the seafood, salt and peperoncino and cook gently for several minutes.
Add the tomato and parsley, then the wine. Raise the heat so the alcohol burns off, then reduce it after a few minutes. Leave the sauce over a very low heat.
Cook the rice in salted water for 20 minutes. About 5 minutes before the end of cooking, add the saffron and stir it in well.
As soon as the rice is cooked, drain it, then mix in the seafood and serve immediately. Alternatively, place the rice in a serving dish and top with the sauce. If wished, garnish with a few of the reserved mussel shells so as to look like 'angels' wings'.

Riso con gli angeli (above right)

Calamari di Sergio Manzella

The floor-length windows of the kitchen of Ristorante Primafila open directly onto the harbour of the pretty little town of Terrasini. The restaurant, created from several old fishermen's houses joined together, serves excellent new-wave Sicilian dishes, such as gamberoni with curry spices and rice, as well as more traditional ones. Sergio Manzella is one of the chefs there.

For 2

400g/14oz squid, cut in rings
2 tbsp olive oil
2 tbsp white wine
1 tsp 'strattu or 2 tsp tomato paste
150ml/5floz fish stock
4 tsp capers
chopped parsley, to garnish

Quickly sauté the squid in some hot oil. Drain off any excess oil.
Add the white wine and let it evaporate for a minute.
Stir the 'strattu or tomato paste into the fish stock, then add it to the squid along with the capers.
Bring the mixture to the boil and simmer it for a few minutes until the sauce thickens.
Serve sprinkled with parsley, '*Not* basil. We *never* put *basil* on fish!'

Intense concentration

'Strattu or *estratto* is a blood-red tomato paste laid out on boards to harden and darken like the brutal aftermath of a shoot-out under the infernal southern sun.

In the markets of Sicily, especially in the east, you sometimes see 'strattu for sale, piled high in rusty pyramids, scooped and sold by the spoonful. It is a vanishing art, this concentration of the tomato into a blood-red paste laid out on boards to harden and darken like the brutal aftermath of a shoot-out under the infernal southern sun.

'Strattu is a distillation of 20kg/45lb of tomatoes into one, with the consistency of clay and far, far richer than ordinary tomato pastes. Salt, perhaps a little basil, is the only condiment. To make it, you need several days of hot sun with little humidity, a slight breeze to speed up the drying and a lot of willing assistants with strong arms. Ripe tomatoes are juiced and seeded, then cooked with salt for about an hour. The purée is left to stand overnight, then passed through a food mill and spread onto large wooden boards or tables in the sun and stirred throughout the day (trickier than it sounds as the purée is inclined to trickle off the tables). As the moisture evaporates, the tomatoes start to thicken. The boards are covered at night and the process repeated for four or five days until the paste turns dark red and shrinks to the extent it becomes like putty. It is kneaded and worked for a further day then packed into ceramic or glass jars and covered with olive oil. Methods vary – some cook the tomatoes whole then sieve and purée them; others don't cook the tomatoes at all.

'Strattu is used in ragu, sauces, stews and to give some healthy colour to an anaemic-looking broth. Only a tiny amount need be used at a time, softened in a little hot water. In *The Oxford Companion to Food*, Alan Davidson suggests that a leap of the imagination could make such a sauce an ancestor of tomato ketchup. However substitution is not recommended; regular tomato paste is a better but still inferior replacement.

Sicilian meat cookery

An old Sicilian tale urges Christians to eat beef because God blessed the oxen that sheltered baby Jesus in the manger, as opposed to the donkey that made a racket all night long! Beef, however, was a luxury most Sicilians were unable to enjoy. As the 19th-century Sicilian writer Giovanni Verga wrote, 'It is a feast day when we treat ourselves to meat with our macaroni.'

The climate and poor grazing land made cattle rearing difficult; cattle were exploited to the utmost for work in the fields, and when sent for slaughter made tough eating. Only the rich families could afford quality meat and employ the chefs who had the elaborate techniques with which to cook it. Everyone else had to be content with cheap cuts of inferior quality and offal.

Farsumagru, a dish that is said to date back to the 13th-century Angevin occupation and is named after the French *farce* or stuffing, was originally a thin piece of meat rolled around a breadcrumb filling. In later centuries, the fillings became increasingly elaborate, including eggs, peas, cheese, ham, minced beef, currants and pine nuts and more, until the dish achieved its present status as a complex showpiece for special occasions. *Involtini*, skewered meat or veal rolls with a filling, are more usually found on a daily basis, but depend on the meat being cut more finely than is commonly found in British butchers' shops.

In contemporary Sicily, beefsteak, even when it is as tough as old boots and more expensive than Gucci, is a status symbol enjoyed as soon as anyone has the wherewithal to do so. The first reports of BSE or 'mad cow disease' in Europe, however, immediately prompted nearly every Sicilian family to stop eating beef, temporarily closing butchers' shops around the island. No Sicilian ever takes a knowing chance with his or her food, fanatical as they are about quality and health.

In something of a contradiction, however, eating habits are also influenced by American lifestyles – burger outlets are increasingly ubiquitous, spit-roast chickens widely available and every middle-class mother goes to great lengths to feed her children white chicken breasts. Turkey is traditionally eaten in Palermo on November 11th, the Feast of San Martino. Rabbit and game are commonly found in country areas, although there is little of the latter left to be hunted. Lamb, mutton and

'It is a feast day when we treat ourselves to meat with our macaroni.' GIOVANNI VERGA

castrato, the meat of a young castrated ram or goat, are also popular. Veal is mostly used for meatballs, stuffings and escalopes.

Pork was traditionally a winter meat, and country families kept a pig that could be raised at little cost, fattened on prickly pears, acorns and the water left over from cooking pasta. Lard was once widely used as a cooking fat, but the heat generally prevented Sicilians from developing a wide range of *salumi*. The exception that proves the rule is the splendid Salame di Sant'Angelo di Brolo, from Messina.

After only seven years of discussion and debate, a group of local producers got together to form a consortium to promote this *salame*, which originated at the time of the 11th-century Norman conquest of this part of Sicily. Banned by the Arabs, production was resumed in the 16th century and production has changed little; the main difference is that demand has now grown to the extent that pigmeat has to be imported from elsewhere in Italy. Unusually, different pork cuts are cut into cubes by hand using razor-sharp knives, flavoured with sea salt and grains of pepper to make a unique *prosciutto*-cum-*salame*, air-dried in the cool, pure mountain air of the Nebrodie Mountains.

Lamb cutlets with pistachio pesto

For 4
8 lamb cutlets
olive oil
50g/2oz pistachios
50g/2oz breadcrumbs
grated zest of 2 lemons
salt
peperoncino or black pepper

Preheat the grill. Lightly oil the grill pan and the lamb cutlets.
Finely chop the pistachios in a food processor, then mix with the breadcrumbs, zest and seasoning. Add enough olive oil to bind the mixture without letting it become soggy.
Grill the cutlets – the exact time will depend on how thick they are, how hot your grill is and how well you like them cooked, but approximately 5 minutes on each side.
When almost ready, take the chops from the grill and slather over the pistachio mixture to make a thick crusty topping. Flash under the grill for 1 minute or until the topping starts to brown and crisp.

Variation
Make an almond-olive pesto using finely chopped almonds, olives, basil, lemon juice, olive oil and seasonings.

Lamb cutlets with salmoriglio sauce

For 4
125ml/4floz olive oil
125ml/4floz hot water
2 tbsp lemon juice
1 clove garlic, halved
1 tsp oregano
1 tbsp chopped fresh parsley
salt
8 lamb cutlets

Pour the oil into a saucepan and gradually whisk in the hot water.
Add the lemon juice, garlic, oregano, parsley and salt to taste.
Place over a medium-low heat, or in a bain-marie, and stir for 5 minutes until the sauce is creamy and smooth. Do not let it boil. Remove the garlic just before serving.
Grill the cutlets under a hot grill and serve with the sauce.

Lamb cutlets with pistachio pesto (left)

Lamb, fennel & orange casserole

For 4
2 fennel bulbs, sliced
olive oil
125g/4oz pancetta, cubed
4 shallots, chopped
2 garlic cloves, chopped
900g/2lb lamb shoulder, cubed
4 large tomatoes, skinned, deseeded and chopped
2 tbsp 'strattu or 1 tbsp tomato paste
125ml/4floz white wine
300ml/10floz stock
100g/3½oz green olives, chopped
salt and pepper
a large pinch of dried oregano
zest and juice of 1 orange
fresh parsley, chopped

Lightly steam or boil the fennel and set aside.
Heat a little oil in a large casserole over a medium heat and brown the pancetta, shallots and garlic. Raise the heat slightly, then add the lamb and brown on all sides.
Add the tomatoes and 'strattu, stir briefly then add the white wine. Let it reduce for a few minutes, then pour in the stock.
Bring to the boil and simmer for 10 minutes.
Add the fennel, olives, salt, pepper and dried oregano. Cover and cook for about 1 hour or until the lamb is tender.
Stir in the orange zest and juice, cook for 5 more minutes then serve with freshly chopped parsley.

Pork or lamb steaks with red wine

For 4

4 pork or lamb steaks
olive oil
salt
peperoncino or black pepper
50ml/2floz red wine
2 tsp fennel seeds, lightly crushed
juice of 1 lemon

Marinate the meat in olive oil, salt and peperoncino or black pepper for at least an hour.

Heat a little fresh oil in a heavy frying pan and quickly brown the steaks on both sides over a high heat.

Reduce the heat, add the wine and fennel seeds, and simmer for 4–5 minutes on each side until the meat is cooked and the wine has mostly evaporated.

Sprinkle the lemon juice over the meat before serving, along with any juices left in the pan.

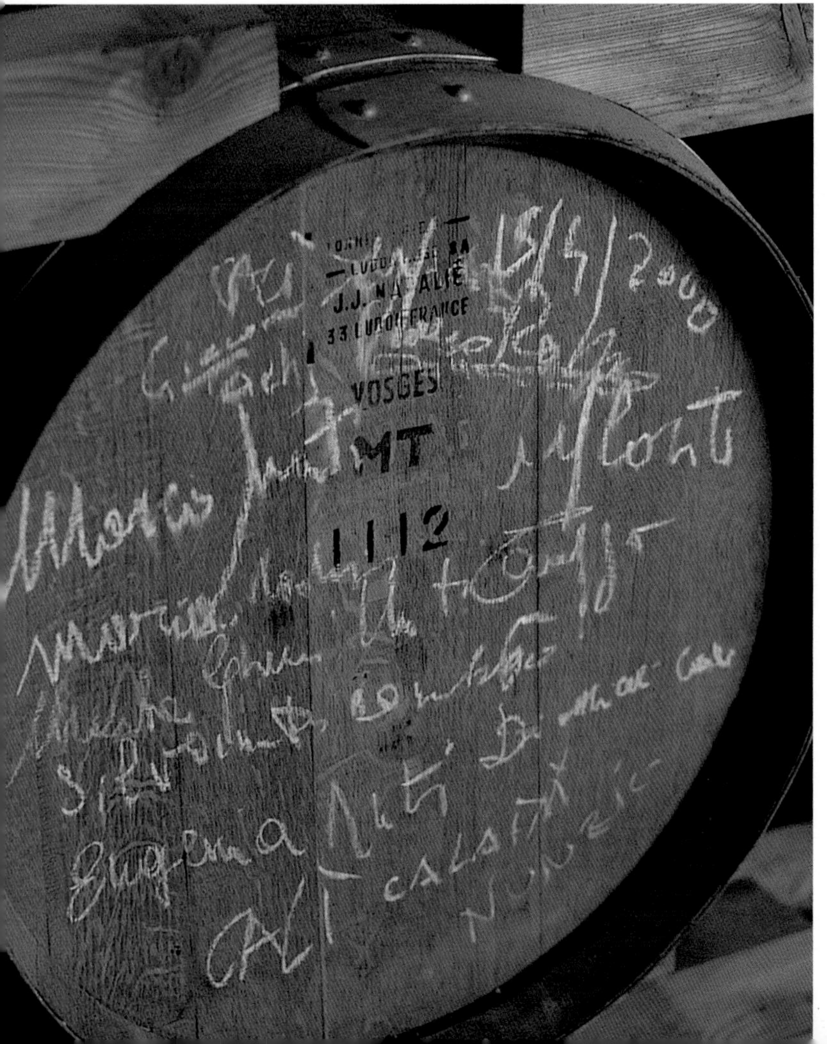

Angelo Treno's pork with prunes

At his elegantly rustic restaurant Al Fogher, on the outskirts of Piazza Armerina, Angelo Treno is passionate about preserving local ingredients and traditions but also draws on a broader European sensibility. The day I visited, he served hot Piacentino saffron cheese with peppercorn and honey sauce, broad bean potage with wheatberries and wild greens, tongue with candied fruit, raisins and pine nuts, and this French-influenced pork dish.

For 4

1kg–1.5kg /2lb 4oz–3lb boned pork joint, preferably tenderloin
Dijon mustard
olive oil
2 sprigs rosemary
5 juniper berries, crushed
4 cloves garlic, crushed
3–4 dried porcini mushrooms
4 shallots, chopped
2 sticks celery, diced
10 soaked or ready-to-eat prunes or mi-cuit plums, chopped
2 tomatoes, skinned, deseeded and chopped
red or white wine or water
salt
peperoncino or black pepper (optional)
Marsala

Preheat the oven to 180°C/350°F/Gas Mark 4. Smear the pork joint with mustard.

Heat about 2 tbsp of olive oil in a casserole and lightly brown the pork on all sides. Add the rosemary, juniper and garlic.

Cover and transfer to the oven to bake for 1 hour 30 minutes to 2 hours (allow 30 minutes per 450g/1lb, plus 30 minutes).

Meanwhile, soak the porcini in a little warm water for 10 minutes. Drain, reserving the liquid, and chop.

About 10 minutes before the joint is ready, gently sauté the shallots in 1 tbsp of oil until they soften, then add the celery and sauté for several more minutes.

Add the prunes, tomatoes, porcini and reserved soaking liquid and cook for 5 minutes over a medium heat.

Remove the pork from the casserole and keep warm; it needs to stand for 10–15 minutes before serving.

Pour off any fat in the casserole, then swish a little wine or water around the pan and let it bubble for 1–2 minutes.

Sieve the pan juices into the prune sauce. Check the seasoning, add a good glug of Marsala and cook for 1–2 minutes more.

Slice the pork and serve covered with a ladleful of sauce.

Anelletti al forno di Linda Ruggiero

In Sicily, Christmas starts on December 8th, the day of the Immaculate Conception and lasts until Epiphany, January 6th. During this period everyone plays cards like mad, keeping up their strength with hearty dishes such as *farsumagru* and this popular baked pasta made with anelletti, a small ring-shaped pasta that is hard to find outside Sicily. In this recipe you can substitute any short, stubby pasta shape, for example penne. Linda generously allowed me to cook this dish alongside her in the kitchen of her 19th-century villa and guesthouse in Terrasini.

For 6–8

1 stick celery
1 large carrot
2 red onions or 4 shallots
olive oil
400g/14oz minced beef
1 glass white wine
3 x 700g/1lb9oz jars tomato passata
salt
450g/1lb fresh or frozen peas
peperoncino or black pepper
2 large aubergines
breadcrumbs
100g/4oz pecorino or Parmesan cheese, grated
600g/1lb5oz anelletti
250–300g/9–11oz buffalo mozzarella, sliced
fresh basil

Finely chop the celery, carrot and onion in a food processor.
Heat just enough olive oil to cover the bottom of a large pan and add the minced vegetables. Fry over a high heat for 10 minutes, stirring continuously so they do not scorch.
Add the minced beef and stir over a high heat until it browns.
Reduce the heat and add the white wine. Once it has evaporated, raise the heat again and add the passata plus half a jar of water. Salt well and leave uncovered on a low heat to simmer.
After 20 minutes, add the peas and cook for another 20 minutes. Season with peperoncino or freshly ground black pepper.
Cut the aubergine into even-sized cubes. Place in a colander and sprinkle lightly with salt. Toss and leave to stand for 10 minutes.
Heat 5cm/2in of olive oil in another pan. Fry the aubergines, without rinsing off the salt, until golden brown. Set aside.
Put a large pan of salted water on to boil for the pasta.
Place a little tomato sauce at the bottom of a wide, shallow cake tin or ovenproof dish. Sprinkle with breadcrumbs and a handful of the grated cheese. Set aside.
Preheat the oven to 200°C/400°F/Gas 6.
Half-cook the pasta. Drain and shake well so no water clings to it.
Stir a ladle of sauce at a time into the drained pasta until it is coated but not too liquidy. There should be some sauce left over. Toss in two handfuls of the grated cheese.
Spread some pasta over the bottom of the prepared tin, then cover with some of the remaining sauce. Add a layer of mozzarella, then a layer of fried aubergines. Layer with more pasta, sauce, mozzarella, and aubergines until finished.
Sprinkle the top with grated cheese and breadcrumbs. (Up to this point the dish can be prepared the night before and refrigerated. Reheating does not harm it, although it tends to make the finished dish a lot firmer.)
Bake for 30 minutes, then remove the dish from the oven and leave it to rest for 10 minutes before turning out.
Garnish with fresh basil leaves and serve. Any leftover sauce can be used for other pasta dishes.

Meatballs with white wine, lemon & bay leaves

There are hundreds of variations for *polpette* or meatballs in Sicily, as they are one of the best ways of making a little piece of tough meat both palatable and go a long way. One particularly refined and elaborate recipe with almonds, pistachios, pine nuts and cinnamon comes from Mazzarino, a medieval hamlet founded by the princes of Butera in the centre of the island and noted for beautiful churches, a ruined castle and friars accused of Mafia involvement. Under cross-examination they admitted to writing blackmail and extortion notes 'but only because the mafiosi were illiterate and did not own a typewriter'. Which has nothing to do with this recipe, but is a fascinating example of Sicilian logic.

For 2

250g/9oz minced beef, veal or pork, or a mix of one part pork to two parts veal
50g/2oz grated pecorino cheese
50g/2oz dried breadcrumbs
4 tbsp chopped fresh parsley
zest and juice of ½ lemon
salt
1 egg
25g/1oz flour
olive oil
1 glass white wine
hot water
4 bay leaves, torn
lemon slices and bay leaves, to garnish

Place the minced meat, grated cheese, breadcrumbs, parsley, lemon zest and salt in a bowl. Mix together with the egg – you can use a wooden spoon, but it's best to do it by hand, and more satisfying to feel the mixture squelching through your fingers.

Form the mixture into small, slightly squashed balls, each about the size of a plum (some Sicilian cooks dip their hands in white wine before they roll out the polpette). Gently roll in the flour until lightly coated all over.

Heat a thin layer of oil in a pan large enough to take all the meatballs without over-crowding. Fry the meatballs over a medium heat for about 10 minutes until nicely browned on both sides. Give them a gentle shake and prod now and then to make sure they're not sticking either to the pan or each other.

Add the wine, turn the heat up a bit, shake the pan so the wine distributes itself fairly evenly, and let the alcohol burn off for a few minutes.

Pour in enough hot water to just cover the meatballs. Add the bay leaves and leave to bubble over a gentle-to-medium heat until the sauce is well reduced and starting to become syrupy.

Add the lemon juice and cook a few minutes more.

Remove the meatballs with a slotted spoon and place in a serving dish. Spoon over some of the sticky pan juices if wished and decorate with whole bay leaves and wafer-thin slices of lemon.

Variation

Simply grill the meatballs and squeeze a little lemon juice over them when cooked.

The spirit of Marsala

There is an almost tangible pull, a tilt in the flat landscape towards Africa, from the shore of Marsala – from the Arabic 'Mars-el-Allah', meaning the port of God. In the heat of the day, the land shimmers, melts and dissolves into the sea.

The Stabilimento Florio museum, *enoteca* and distillery is protected from the winds by high walls surrounding a flower-filled courtyard. From the elegant villa at the top of the long drive, you can see the harbour framed like a painting by the rectangular stone gateway. The palm trees are as high as the sky, and you can taste salt spray on your lips.

Woodhouse, Whitaker, Ingham and Hopps are curiously solid yeoman names to be found in this foreign field, but it was these 18th-century British merchants who started the Marsala trade. Woodhouse, a soap merchant from Liverpool forced ashore during a violent storm, judged that Sicilian wine, when fortified with a bit of strong alcohol, would keep well on long sea voyages. The British Royal Navy became an enthusiastic customer of his new business, and the town started to prosper.

The story is charted in the Florio museum where the sea-level floor is made of tufa, porous local stone strewed with sand, the high vaults are tiled to enable the free circulation of air, and chandeliers give an unexpected touch of gentility. A number of bottles sent to America during Prohibition are ingeniously labelled 'hospital tonic'. The museum also houses swords and rifles left in the *cantine* by Garibaldi when he came ashore in 1860, delighted to find no resistance.

Some years ago, the reputation of this venerable fortified wine plummeted after an ill-judged rush to modernise production propelled by industrial marketing policies. Fortunes have been somewhat revived, thanks to new DOC production rules to remove sickly-sweet extraneous flavours such as egg, banana, cream, coffee and other syrups, plus the dedication of producers such as Marco de Bartoli and Florio. However, it's not all good news; the regulations still allow a multitude of grapes, styles and ages to be sold under the Marsala name. *Caveat emptor.*

Duck with Marsala

An adaptation of a classic *monzù* recipe, this dish was originally made using wild duck.

For 4
6 slices sandwich bread
250ml/8floz Marsala
3 chicken livers
1 small onion
20g/1oz parsley
2 sage leaves
50g/2oz breadcrumbs
½ tsp ground cloves
salt and black pepper
olive oil
2 ducks, about 1kg/2lb4oz each, or 1 large one

Preheat the oven to 180°C/350°F/Gas Mark 4. Cut the slices of bread in half and soak in half the Marsala. Set aside.
Finely chop the chicken livers, onions, parsley and sage, then mix together. Add the breadcrumbs, cloves and 2 tbsp of Marsala. Season well and, if the mixture seems dry, moisten with olive oil.
Stuff the ducks with this mixture. Either sew or skewer the cavity and neck to close, then truss. Prick the skin in several places, season with salt and pepper and smear with a little olive oil.
Roast the ducks, allowing 20 minutes per 450g/1lb plus an extra 30 minutes. Half an hour before the end of the calculated cooking time, pour off most of the fat from the roasting pan and tuck the slices of soaked bread around the sides of the birds.
Remove the ducks and bread from the roasting pan and set aside for 10 minutes before carving.
Pour off any remaining fat from the pan, place over a high heat and deglaze the pan with the remaining Marsala.
Strain the sauce into a clean saucepan, bring to the boil and reduce over a high heat until the sauce is thick and syrupy.
Serve each portion of duck with some stuffing, the sauce and a slice of oven-baked bread.

Black chicken or rabbit

This is an old Baroque recipe from eastern Sicily taken from *Sicilia in Boca* by Franca Colonna Romano, hand-printed in 1974 in Sicilian, Italian and English. The book has some curious but endearing transliterations and mangling between the three languages.

For 4
1 chicken or rabbit, cut into portions
500ml/18floz dry white wine
1 medium onion, chopped
4 tbsp olive oil
25g/1oz bitter chocolate, grated
1 tbsp sugar
2 cloves
2 tsp fennel seeds
2 tbsp vinegar
salt
peperoncino or black pepper
potato flour (optional)

Marinate the chicken or rabbit for 2 hours in the wine, turning occasionally. Remove and dry well.
Fry the onion in the olive oil until soft but not coloured. Add the chicken or rabbit and cook until golden brown.
Stir in the chocolate, sugar, cloves, fennel seeds, vinegar, salt and peperoncino. Make sure the meat is well coated with sauce. Cover and cook over a moderate heat for 30–40 minutes.
To quote the English translation: 'If the gravy proves too thin, take out the pieces of rabbit and make it denser with a pinch of instant potato mix.' That means potato flour, not Smash.

Black chicken (right)

Blood red tomatoes

In Corleone, Biagio Salvaggio took me to see the place where he grows superb peaches and tomatoes, quite remarkably without any irrigation at all. The only water comes from rainfall in the cold months, a tribute to the extraordinary fertility of the Sicilian soil. On a January day, the wide mountain plains were exposed to a bitter wind, the rich black earth strewn with green herbs, blankets of marigolds and the occasional streak of bright blue iris.

The area is known for its tomatoes, large and round, sweet and juicy, the size of a man's fist. They are picked from the end of July, and are particularly suited for drying in the burning sun that bleaches the interior of Sicily in the summer.

Each summer, the whole family decamps to the countryside to make the year's supply of tomato sauce. Mary Taylor Simetti in *On Persephone's Island* describes this annual event as the most important domestic ritual of the Sicilian summer, and that 'each housewife believes in the efficacy of her favourite method with fervor equal to that with which she believes in the efficacy of her favourite saint'.

Biagio's wife, Giovanna, favours the old tomatoes-under-the-blanket technique. 'It's a full day's work,' she said. 'We set aside the bottles to warm in the sun, then start to pick the tomatoes which are washed and left to dry in the heat of the day. You slit each one open, remove the seeds, then cook the pulp in a huge cauldron pan over a wood fire. No oil, nothing – just crush the tomatoes down as they cook. When the skin starts to peel, we pass the pulp through a food mill. In the old days this would be done by hand through a large sieve. Now we're modern, we do it by machine! Then you cook it again so it thickens up, adding seasoning and lots of basil. We pour the hot sauce into bottles, put them in a pile, cover them with heavy woollen blankets and leave them for several days; they just keep on cooking, getting stronger and thicker all the time.'

The sauce is used as a base for others. 'You fry a little garlic and onion in oil, then add some *sugo* and a pinch of sugar. Everyone adds sugar to their tomato sauce in Sicily. The tomatoes are naturally sweet, but we like it even sweeter!'

Pachino, at the south eastern tip of Sicily, is also renowned for tomatoes. Nothing stands between the long beaches and the coast of Africa except a single lighthouse, the melancholy atmosphere accentuated by a string of abandoned houses marking the route of a disused railway line going nowhere. Then, as you drive through the low hills you come across a curious, if not downright comical sight: long white tunnels, hundreds of them, leading down to the seashore, the plastic gardens of Pachino, and one of the great market gardens of Sicily.

'The tomatoes are naturally sweet, but we like it even sweeter!' GIOVANNA SALVAGGIO

They grow several sorts of tomato, including an Israeli variety called Naomi that achieves its apotheosis here in Sicily: clusters of little cherries that explode in the mouth with just the right amount of sweetness and a hint of acidity. Larger salad tomatoes of the Marmande-Raf variety are called *costoluto*, ugly, green and red ribbed brutes whose looks belie their erotic taste. A perfect tomato in an imperfect world.

I asked Giacomo Giunta, a local grower, why the tomatoes were so succulent and juicy. 'It's the soil,' he explained, 'the fact it's next to the sea. The saltier the land, the more the tomato reacts by becoming sweeter, which balances out the acidity. It's all to do with the temperature, the sun, the sea and the salt. And the calcium in the soil also makes them nice and firm.'

Pachino tomatoes are much sought-after on the wholesale Italian markets, but the high cost of production means margins are tight. Giacomo was a smart young man, keen to develop business, and wanted to know if people in England would also like sun-dried cherry and *costoluto* tomatoes from Pachino. I promised I would write about how wonderful the tomatoes were, and bit into a tomato as red as the setting sun.

Sautéed rosemary potatoes with cherry tomatoes & black olives

For 4

1kg/2lb 4oz waxy potatoes or good all-rounders
olive oil
2–3 tbsp chopped fresh rosemary
4 large cloves garlic, peeled but left whole
salt
peperoncino or black pepper
12 cherry tomatoes
12 black olives
fresh parsley, chopped

Peel the potatoes and cut into small chunks. Par-boil them for 10 minutes, then drain and blot well to absorb excess moisture.
Heat a thin layer of oil in a frying pan. Add the half-cooked potatoes, rosemary, garlic, a little salt and a lot of peperoncino or black pepper, as much as you can take.
Turn the potatoes around in the oil so that they are well coated, then leave to brown over a medium heat, flipping occasionally. Keep checking to see they aren't burning or sticking.
After 10–15 minutes, when the potatoes are almost golden and crispy-crunchy, throw in the tomatoes and olives and mix gently.
Cook for a few minutes more until the tomatoes start to go limp and the skins look a little charred.
Sprinkle the dish with chopped parsley and serve immediately, removing the garlic cloves if you prefer.

LA SAPIENZA DEL
LATTE
UHT

Cauliflower salad

For 4

- 1 large cauliflower, broken into florets
- 1 large roasted red bell pepper, sliced
- 12 black olives, pitted
- 4 anchovies, chopped
- 2 tbsp capers
- 4 tbsp olive oil
- 2 tbsp lemon juice
- peperoncino or black pepper (optional)
- fresh parsley, chopped

Blanch the cauliflower florets in a large pan of boiling salted water for 2–3 minutes, then drain thoroughly.

Toss the cauliflower while still warm with the bell pepper, olives, anchovies and capers, then mix in the olive oil and lemon juice. Adjust the seasoning to taste.

Sprinkle with chopped parsley and leave to cool. Chill the salad for several hours before serving.

Broccoli braised with red wine

In this flexible cooked salad, the broccoli can be replaced with cauliflower, and the anchovies or olives left out altogether.

For 2

- 250g/9oz broccoli
- shavings of pecorino cheese
- ½ red onion, chopped
- 6 black olives, chopped
- 6 anchovies, chopped
- peperoncino or black pepper
- olive oil
- ½ glass red wine
- fresh parsley, chopped

Break the broccoli into florets and place a layer in the bottom of a saucepan. Sprinkle with some of the pecorino, red onion, olives and anchovies, then repeat the layers.

Season with peperoncino or pepper and drizzle with olive oil.

Cover and simmer very gently until very soft, stirring occasionally.

Add the red wine, turn up the heat and simmer for a few minutes to evaporate any excess liquid.

Serve sprinkled with parsley – this helps it look more appetising, but this dish, while delicious, will never win any beauty parades.

Blood orange, fennel, olive & smoked herring salad (top right)

Blood orange, fennel, olive & smoked herring salad

This makes a good antipasto or buffet dish.

For 4

- 2 large blood oranges
- 1 fennel bulb, finely sliced, or 1 red onion
- about 12 black or green olives, pitted if desired
- 125g/4oz smoked herring, cut into pieces (optional)
- olive oil
- lemon juice
- salt
- peperoncino or black pepper

Peel and segment the oranges, discarding the membrane, then dice the flesh and place it in a bowl along with any juice.

Add the fennel or red onion, olives and smoked herring, if using.

Pour over some olive oil, add a squeeze of lemon juice and mix together. Season, and mix again before serving.

Melon & black fig salad

For 2

1 canteloupe, ogen or other ripe melon

2 ripe black figs

4 tbsp Marsala

1 tbsp toasted almonds

Cut the melon into quarters and discard the seeds. Remove the skin and cut the flesh into chunks. Place in a bowl.

Slice or quarter the figs and toss them with the melon.

Mix the Marsala into the fruit and refrigerate the salad for several hours or overnight.

Before serving cold or at room temperature, sprinkle the fruit salad with the toasted almonds.

Melon & black fig salad (right)

Stuffed peaches

Leonforte, like most Sicilian hill towns, has its share of treasures. The monumental Palazzo Branciforte can be seen from miles off. There's a handsome fountain, built of gold-coloured stone, with 24 spouts, and a tiny circular piazza with zigzag escalier. But it remains a small country town going about its business of producing a giant broad bean and a delectable, late-maturing peach know as *la pesca tardiva di Leonforte*.

In summer the orchards have a singular appearance. At first sight, it could be a crop of white paper bags. In fact it is a costly, labour-intensive but time-honoured agricultural technique in which each fruit is individually 'bagged' in late June and left until ripe and ready to be picked by hand in early autumn.

Greeny-yellow in colour, the peaches have a thin, fuzzy skin. The flesh is firm, yellow, fragrant and clings to the stone. They are the sort of peaches angels eat in heaven. Local women use them to make wonderful conserve and fruit syrup, but you could spend the rest of your life eating them just as they are, the juice running down your chin as you gaze across the gold and purple mountains of the Madonie.

For 4

1 tbsp raisins or currants

2 tsp Marsala or brandy

6 large, ripe peaches

4 savoiardi biscuits or sponge fingers, crushed

50g/2oz sugar, plus 2 tbsp extra

1 egg yolk

1 tsp unsweetened cocoa powder

1 tsp ground cinnamon

40g/1½oz butter, softened and diced, plus extra for greasing

1 glass dry white wine

Preheat the oven to 200°C/400°F/Gas 6. Meanwhile, soak the dried fruit in the Marsala or brandy for 20 minutes.

Cut the peaches in half and take out the stone. Spoon out a little of the flesh to enlarge the cavity, then chop the extracted pulp.

Mix the pulp well with the crushed biscuits, sugar, egg yolk, cocoa, cinnamon, the drained dried fruit and half the butter.

Arrange the peaches cut-side up in a greased ovenproof serving dish and fill each one with the biscuit mixture.

Top each peach half with a knob of butter and sprinkle with the extra sugar. Pour the wine over and between the peaches.

Bake the peaches for 30 minutes, then serve hot or cold.

Gelo di melone

Watermelon pudding

Watermelon gives this chilled pudding a very oriental feel and colour – think 1001 nights rather than hot water bottles. It is a traditional Palermo favourite during the three-day Feast of Santa Rosalia in July. The chocolate chips represent watermelon seeds.

If you have a good supply of unsprayed jasmine flowers, steep them in a little water for a day before making the jelly, then strain and add the fragrant water to the watermelon juice.

The use of cornflour is most authentic, however arrowroot gives the pudding a better texture and appearance.

For 4

1 large watermelon
50g/2oz cornflour or arrowroot
50g/2oz sugar
1 cinnamon stick
a few drops of vanilla extract (optional)
chocolate chips or shavings, candied peel, finely chopped pistachios, ground cinnamon, fresh jasmine flowers, or any combination to decorate

Slice the watermelon then cut the flesh into chunks. Put the melon through a juice extractor. Alternatively, whizz in a food processor, then sieve, or use the traditional method which is to press the fruit with a broad wooden spoon through a sieve. You will need 1 litre/1¾ pints of juice.

Dissolve the sugar in the juice – depending on the sweetness of the watermelon, you may not need it all. Then sift in the cornflour or arrowroot, stirring well to prevent lumps.

Transfer the mixture to a saucepan and add the cinnamon stick and vanilla, if using. Place over a medium-low heat and bring slowly to boiling point, stirring constantly as it thickens.

Lower the heat, keep stirring, and cook for a further 2–3 minutes, then remove from the heat and discard the cinnamon stick.

Pour the mixture into a wetted mould or individual serving dishes and leave to cool, then chill for several hours

Decorate with suitably Moorish sensuality before serving.

Gelo di melone

Gelo di limone

Lemon jelly

The scent of a bowl of Sicilian lemons can fill a room. Many old recipes simply instruct the cook to use a lemon from the garden, picked from dark-green trees such as those in the grounds of the old villa near Cinisi, bowing their heavy branches to the ground.

The lemons were organically grown by two young brothers, Giuseppe and Ettore Cracchiolo, who started farming sustainably several years ago, motivated both by economic necessity and ideological conviction.

Beehives provide honey, and a natural pollination system. The trees benefit from pure mountain water, the wonderful growing climate, long hours of light and good, rich soil. Pruning is the hardest part. 'You can actually kill the tree if you do it incorrectly, but all our trees have been perfectly pruned!' they add with a typically Sicilian blend of innocence and *braggadocio*.

Ironically, although the brothers now sell their sweetly perfumed lemons and other organic produce to markets abroad, their is no local demand. 'Sicilians won't pay the extra price for organic lemons, they just don't see the need.'

For 4

20g/¾oz leaf gelatine
750ml/1 pint 7floz water
400g/14oz sugar
zest of 2 lemons
250ml/9floz fresh lemon juice
2–3 tbsp limoncello (optional)
lemon slices and leaves, to decorate, or red berries, or hundreds and thousands

Soak the gelatine for 5 minutes in 2–3 tablespoons of the water.

Heat the remaining water and sugar gently until the sugar dissolves. Raise the heat and add the soaked gelatine, stirring until dissolved. The water should be very hot but not boiling.

Remove from the heat, add the lemon zest, juice and liqueur (if using) and pour into a wetted mould or – far safer – individual serving glasses that do not require you to turn the jelly out.

Leave to cool, then chill in the fridge for several hours.

Decorate with slices of lemon and leaves, or with some red berries. Or, in true Sicilian style, with hundreds and thousands: less sophisticated but more fun.

Riso nero

This is an authentic Messinese dish dedicated to their own miracle-working, Byzantine Black Madonna of Tindari.

For 6–8

1 litre/1 pint 15floz full-fat milk
75g/3oz caster sugar
several strips of lemon peel
a few drops of vanilla extract
500g/1lb 2oz pudding rice
a pinch of salt
1 cinnamon stick
300g/10oz unsweetened cocoa
200g/7oz bitter chocolate, grated
200g/7oz chopped almonds, toasted
4 demi-tasse cups strong espresso coffee
a large knob of butter
100g/4oz candied fruit, chopped
whipped cream, to serve

Place the milk, sugar, lemon peel and vanilla extract in a large saucepan and bring to scalding point – the moment when it starts to make a ring of lacy bubbles around the edge of the pan.

Stir in the rice, salt and cinnamon stick. Cover and cook gently, stirring occasionally, for 20 minutes or until the rice is cooked and all the milk has been absorbed.

Remove from the heat and discard the cinnamon and lemon peel.

Add the cocoa gradually, mixing well after each addition.

Stir in the grated chocolate, almonds and espresso and mix until all the grains turn a mahogany colour.

Fold in the butter, then transfer to a serving dish.

Decorate the pudding with the chopped candied fruit and serve hot or cold with whipped cream to accompany.

Cannoli di Linda Ruggiero

To say that *cannoli* and *cassata* are the iconic sweets of Sicily is an understatement. Delicious as they are, it is hard for a non-Sicilian to fully appreciate the social and emotional significance with which they are invested. A 17th-century Palermitano poet once warbled they were 'the sceptre of kings and the rod of Moses'.

Cannoli can vary in size from doll-size to the outsize versions made by the Albanian Sicilians of Piana degli Albanesi. Ricotta is the common element. *Canna* is cane, as in sugar cane, and also means the barrel of a gun. According to food writer Waverley Root, *cannoli* are very ancient and their phallic shape is thought to go back to prehistory.

Linda uses traditional cane moulds made of cane. You may be able to source metal ones through specialist kitchenware shops. Eat *cannoli* with your hands – if you try to cut one with a fork it will probably spin right off the plate and across the table.

To make about 24

FOR THE CANNOLI SHELLS

300g/10oz flour
1 glass white wine
25g/1oz butter, melted
15g/½oz unsweetened cocoa
1 tbsp sugar
1 tsp ground coffee
a pinch of salt
1 egg white, lightly beaten
oil or lard for deep-frying

FOR THE FILLING

1kg/2lb4oz ricotta
500g/1lb2oz caster sugar
50g/2oz bitter chocolate chips
vanilla icing sugar
candied orange peel, glacé cherries or other glacé fruit (optional)

Combine the flour, wine, melted butter, cocoa, sugar, coffee and salt to form a dough. Shape into a ball and leave to rest for 1 hour.

Meanwhile, make the filling. In an electric mixer, beat the ricotta and sugar thoroughly for 10–15 minutes until smooth. Stir in the chocolate chips.

Roll out the dough (either by hand or using a pasta machine) to give wafer-thin rectangles 10–13cm/4–5in wide.

Fold the bottom left hand corner of the rectangle diagonally back on itself to give a triangle, then use a ravioli cutter to cut the paste across the top half of the triangle (the ravioli cutter gives a frilly edge). Repeat, working your way up each of the pastry rectangles until all the dough is used up.

Fold each triangle around a cannoli mould and brush the join with egg white to seal, but avoid getting any on the mould itself.

Heat the oil or lard to 190°C/375°F and deep-fry the cannoli, still on the moulds, one or two at a time. Prod with a spoon to turn over. If the pastry starts to look like bubblewrap, it's going right. The cannoli only take about 1 minute to cook, so don't wander off.

Lift out the cannoli with a large fork or tongs and stand them upright to drain in a bowl lined with kitchen paper. When they are cool enough to handle, slip them off the moulds.

You can make the filling in advance, but fill the cannoli only just before serving. The shells will keep in an airtight box for 10 days.

Spoon some ricotta filling into each shell and sprinkle with the vanilla icing sugar. If wished, decorate the ends with candied orange peel or glacé fruit. Be careful however: in Sicily this is a controversy you engage in at your peril.

The best cassata in Sicily

'No one decorates *cassata* the way we do. We make *cassata* Sicilians dream about.'

The secret of a good *cassata*, the rich Sicilian layered cake, is the ricotta, said Signor Vito Palazzolo. 'The Roman and Sardinian ricottas aren't bad, but they're not like ours! And no one decorates *cassata* the way we do. We make *cassata* Sicilians dream about.'

Although officially retired, Signor Palazzolo is usually to be found at the family store in Cinisi, near Palermo. The lustrous, marble palace to *pasticceria* was founded by his father Santi in 1920. Now another Santi runs the business, Vito's son, President of the Pastry Chefs Association of Sicily and one of only two Sicilian members of the Master Pastry Chefs of Italy. Under the shop, also renowned for its ice cream, a small army of pastry chefs turn out a fabulous selection of Technicolor cakes and pastries. As well as the Cinisi shop, the family have another in Palermo Airport.

The Palazzolo *cassata* is indeed a splendid sight, the *pan di Spagna* sponge a mere backdrop for the luscious, slightly sharp ewes' milk *crema di ricotta*, the almond paste coloured green (a substitute for the original pistachio paste) and snow white icing topped with jewel-like glacé fruit. *Cassata* is sold by the weight; the more fruit, the costlier it will be. Few make *cassata* at home anymore; apart from the necessary skill, it looks more impressive, and shows respect (because you've spent more money), to offer one from a famous *pasticceria* to guests instead.

Cassata Siciliana – not to be confused with the frozen ice cream cake called *cassata gelata* – is said to take its name from the Arabic *quas'at*, the sloping mould in which it was made. Some suggest the name is a derivation of the Latin *caseo* (cheese) from which the *cassata* was made; still others insist, with equal certainty, it is because the cake is *incassato*, packed into a tin for construction. Either way, by the 16th century the cake had become so popular the nuns of the Convent of Mazara del Vallo had to be temporarily banned from making them when, in an effort to keep up with demand, they simply neglected to fulfil their religious duties.

Back to the present – and Signor Palazzolo's monologue on modern times: 'These days you have to keep creating new things, but I'm sad that fewer people want the old recipes such as *taralli* (fennel seed biscuits) anymore. Maybe they look a bit plain alongside all the fancy ones, but I suppose in the old days hunger made everything look good. And I'll tell you another thing: the bread today tastes like rubber bands and then it's hard by the next morning! Come on, have some *buccellato* – there are 20 different ingredients in the filling. My father won the world prize for this in 1925. Here, try our *panettone*,' he said, suddenly switching tracks. 'Delicious,' I said. 'Better than I've had in Milan.' No reply, just a slight, Sicilian lift of the eyebrow. He didn't need to be told.

Cassata

TO MAKE A 20CM/8IN CAKE

FOR THE PAN DI SPAGNA SPONGE

175g/6oz sugar
6 large eggs, separated
2 tbsp lemon juice
a few drops of vanilla extract
1 tsp baking powder
a pinch of salt
150g/5oz flour, sifted
4 tbsp Marsala

FOR THE RICOTTA FILLING

600g/1lb 5oz ricotta, preferably ewes' milk
100g/4oz caster sugar
vanilla extract
200g/8oz candied peel
50g/2oz plain chocolate
juice and grated zest of 1 orange

FOR THE MARZIPAN

200g/8oz ground almonds
200g/8oz sugar
green colouring
water
icing sugar, for rolling

FOR THE DECORATION

300g/10oz icing sugar
1½ tbsp lemon juice
100g/4oz glacé fruit, or more, to decorate

Preheat the oven to 180°C/350°F/Gas Mark 4. Butter and flour a spring-form cake tin.

Make the pan di Spagna by beating the sugar, egg yolks, lemon juice, vanilla and baking powder together in a large bowl until the mixture starts to thicken and the sugar dissolves.

In another bowl, beat the egg whites and salt together until snowy peaks form. Fold them gently into the yolk mixture, then fold in the flour a little at a time until the batter is smooth.

Turn the batter carefully into the cake tin and bake for 40 minutes or until puffed and golden. Cool on a rack for 15 minutes before loosening the sides of the tin and cooling further.

When the cake is completely cold, slice it into three discs and sprinkle each with Marsala until moistened but not drenched.

In an electric mixer, beat the ricotta and sugar for 10–15 minutes until smooth. Stir in the rest of the filling ingredients and set aside.

To make the marzipan, mix the almonds, sugar and colouring together with just enough water to make a paste. It needs to be on the dry side, but still soft and pliable. Knead briefly to help release the oils, then set aside.

To assemble, the cassata, line a clean spring-form cake tin, bottom and sides, with plastic wrap, allowing it to fully overhang at the sides. Place the best-looking layer of sponge at the bottom as this will be the top of the finished cake.

Dust the marzipan with icing sugar and roll it out a little. Cut it into strips the height of the tin, then line the sides of the tin with a ring of marzipan, using your hands to smooth it around the sides.

Spread half the ricotta mixture over the sponge in the tin, then cover with another layer of sponge. Spread the rest of the ricotta mixture on top and cover with the final sponge disc.

Cover the cake with plastic wrap and lay a plate on top to act as a weight. Chill for at least 1 hour.

Invert the cake onto a serving dish. Make an icing by mixing the icing sugar, lemon juice and a splash of water together until smooth. Spread the icing over the top of the cassata.

Decorate the cake with glacé fruit, arranged in the form of flowers and petals. Chill for at least another 2 hours before serving.

Merenda

Palermo street food & markets

At the entrance to the teeming Capo market, near the newly renovated Teatro Massimo opera house of *Godfather* fame and symbol of Palermo's rebirth as a great European city, a street seller with a prickly pear stubble was doing a roaring trade. Surrounded by an appreciative male audience, he slipped his hand inside a straw basket covered with a cloth, to produce, like rabbits from a hat, steaming fistfuls of cooked offal to slap onto sesame seed buns. From afar, his customers looked as if they were genuflecting, bending forward to avoid grease spots on their jackets and ties.

The souk-like alleys of the market, one of four in central Palermo, are theatrically hemmed in by gangrenous, decaying tenements: buildings randomly display missing rooms, absent ceilings or the loss of an entire floor. Impossible tangles of wires and cables dangle like festive decorations.

Yet, in autumn, there are fresh green olives, bright and hard, pink flushed garlic, potatoes stacked in perfect size and order or sold boiled along with roasted onions for salads. And all the fruits of Sicily as depicted on the Roman mosaics of Piazza Armerina. It was the richest of produce in the poorest of settings, and reminded me that the Sicilian artist Renato Guttuso had drawn the original stark, unsentimental illustrations for Elizabeth David's book *Italian Food*.

The picture of a favourite saint is wrapped around a weighing scale on a fish stall. The heavy make-up of the brassy assistant is accentuated by the naked lightbulbs of stalls packed so tight that their awnings filter out the brilliant light. You pass a shrine encircled by fresh flowers, then a building with its innards exposed to view. The market is the guts of the city, as well as its heart.

Inside a nearby church, the air was oppressive with the smell of waxed candles, flowers and damp plaster. They say there is a network of tunnels here, built as meeting places for priests and their lovers. We passed stalls selling skinned ox feet with nails

La Dolce Uva
di Mazzarrone

intact, boiled tongues and bunches of sausages tied with raffia. Baby goats in their furry coats hung by their necks. A man was excising the brains out of a skull. The cheapest of cuts, the most obscure and esoteric parts of every animal, are boiled together and served to local shoppers. The best place, however, to sample the Palermo speciality, *pani cu' la meusa* (beef lung and spleen sandwiches) is the Antica Focacceria di San Francesco on the edge of the old Arab-Norman Kalsa district, founded in 1834 and once patronised by Garibaldi, Pirandello and Lucky Luciano. The shop is located opposite the lovely Gothic church of the same name. High ceilings, bow windows, original marble fittings, coloured glass doors and wrought-iron chairs give it a Spanish feel. The great cast iron and brass range roaring away under the central counter was, until recently, wood-fired, but now runs on bottled gas.

Behind the counter the soft bread rolls, *guasteddi*, are filled with warmed ricotta (in the microwave, another sign of the times), slivers of offal scooped from a vat filled with simmering lard, a little salt and, as a final touch, caciocavallo cheese grated with what looks like a two-handed hacksaw. The rolls are expressively termed *schiettu* or 'nubile' when filled with offal only, *maritatu* when accompanied by the cheese; they are chewy and greasy, though not unpalatable, a taste you could learn to crave once a year.

'The stalls are packed so tight that their awnings filter out the brilliant light.'

Panelle are fritters made from chickpea flour, usually eaten in a soft roll. Of probable North African origin, they are a reminder that Tunis is geographically closer than Rome. Although increasingly served in restaurants as part of an antipasto, they are frequently bought either from street vendors (frequently stationed near school gates in the way you might find an ice cream van in England) or from the *friggitoria*, fry shop, where they also sell *arancine, cazzilli, fritto misto*, and *quaglie*, which are small aubergines deep-fried whole and split open to resemble quail tail feathers. Sensible Sicilians only buy *frittura* straight out of the pan.

On our way to the coast, in search of freshly boiled octopus, the colour of Englishmen left too long out in the sun, we screeched to a halt somewhere in the Palermo suburbs. At a makeshift roadside stand kebabs, another legacy of Arabic rule, were glowing over a charcoal brazier. The vendor whipped them off the skewer onto a piece of greaseproof paper, added some salt and a squeeze of lemon. It smelled good, looked like chunks of chicken breast but tasted more savoury, chewier and slightly fatty. 'Brava!' roared Michele, who had been watching my reaction closely. 'Now, you eat like a real Palermitana!' Real Palermitani, of course, eat *stigghiole*, kid or lamb intestines.

Back in the city centre, the first hint of winter had come with the appearance of the chestnut sellers on the street. Each had a tall, chimney-like contraption with charcoal in the bottom and a pan on top billowing steam. Michele said they used slow-burning, old railway sleepers for fuel. As we walked through the Piazza Castelnuovo, newly made over with a pavement studded with tiny, inset lights, Rosy's attention was distracted by another fast-food vendor. 'That's wonderful! Something I had never thought I would see in Palermo – I have to go get one.' It was a New York Hot Dog stand.

Cazzilli

These deep-fried potato croquettes have the popular nickname of little pricks. Making *cazzilli* is not difficult but takes a bit of practice. As Rosy says, 'They sound easy, but if you don't get them just right they go soggy or heavy; when they're good, they're crisp on the outside, melting inside.'

Makes about 12
500g/1lb 2oz potatoes, peeled
1 egg, plus 1 egg yolk
50g/2oz caciocavallo or pecorino, grated
2 tbsp chopped fresh parsley
1 tbsp fennel seeds (optional)
salt
breadcrumbs or flour
oil for deep-frying

Boil the potatoes in salted water until tender, then drain and either mash well or pass through a mouli or potato ricer.
Mix with the whole egg, egg yolk, cheese, parsley, fennel seeds and salt. The mixture can be left overnight at this stage to help firm it up, but if it still seems very loose, add some breadcrumbs.
Oil your hands lightly and form the potato mixture into small cylinders, then coat them in flour or breadcrumbs.
Deep-fry, drain on kitchen paper and serve with an extra sprinkling of sea salt.

'There's always room in your stomach for more' SICILIAN PROVERB

Panelle

Chickpea fritters

Panelle are popular Palermo street snacks of presumed Arab origin. They are also traditionally eaten, along with *arancine* and *cuccia*, a pudding made from wholewheat berries, on December 13th, the feast day of Santa Lucia. On that day, Sicilians avoid all food made with wheat flour in memory of the time they were miraculously saved from famine by the unexpected arrival of a ship laden with wheat. Too famished to wait for the grain to be milled, they cooked it whole.

Makes about 20
250g/9oz chickpea flour
600ml/1 pint water
salt
a handful of parsley leaves, finely chopped
oil for deep-frying
lemon juice
soft bread rolls (optional)

Pour the water into a heavy pan, then steadily whisk in a stream of chickpea flour. Lumps are undesirable.
Add the salt and parsley and cook over a medium-low heat, stirring constantly, until the mixture thickens and pulls away from the side of the pan.
Pour the mixture onto a cold surface, ideally a marble slab, and use a wooden spoon or spatula to spread it out wafer thin. Leave to cool, then cut the paste into small triangles and deep-fry until golden brown.
Sprinkle with lemon juice and eat at once, or sandwich in a bread roll to make *pane con panelle*.

Panelle (right)

Arancine di Giovanna Cavasino

Rice balls

Arancine, or 'little oranges', are a savoury speciality at Il Tulipano in Erice. The locals have an in-built radar that guides them into the shop just at the moment the *arancine* emerge like rusty oranges from the fryer.

Fillings vary around Sicily, as do shapes. As a rough guide, round is for meat sauce, oval for a bechamel-based sauce with ham and cheese, pear-shaped for a chicken sauce, but you can never be quite sure until you take a bite.

Giovanna adds a little chicken stock to the water in which the rice cooks (from a stock cube – like most Sicilian cooks she swears by them). As she described the recipe to me, she became increasingly emphatic: 'Don't drain the rice, it must absorb all the water! And don't overcook it either! And it mustn't stick in the pan!'

The good news is that all stages up to the actual frying can be done in advance and, once cooked, the *arancine* can be reheated in a conventional or microwave oven. The bad news is that bits of rice seem to turn up everywhere in the kitchen for days afterwards.

MAKES ABOUT 16

FOR THE FILLING

1 onion, finely chopped
1 carrot, finely chopped
1 stick celery, finely chopped
500g/1lb2oz minced beef
2 tbsp tomato paste
125ml/4floz white wine
salt
peperoncini or black pepper
200g/7oz frozen peas, defrosted
25g/1oz fresh basil, shredded
olive oil

FOR THE RICE

1.7 litres/3 pints chicken stock or water, or a mixture
600g/1lb 4oz arborio rice
2 tsp saffron strands, soaked in warm water
50g/2oz butter
100g/4oz grated pecorino cheese
2 eggs, beaten
50g/2oz primosale or provolone cheese, cubed

FOR THE COATING

flour
4 eggs, beaten
breadcrumbs
oil for deep-frying

To make the filling, gently fry the onion in some olive oil until it wilts, then add the carrot and celery and fry until soft.

Add the minced beef and cook until brown, stirring often. Add the tomato paste followed by the white wine, salt and peperoncini and simmer for 20 minutes.

Stir in the peas and continue cooking for 5 minutes. Add the basil and turn off the heat. Check the seasoning (it needs to be robust) and leave the mixture to cool.

To make the rice mixture, bring the stock or water to a boil and add the rice and saffron, plus salt to taste. Boil for 15–20 minutes, stirring occasionally until the rice is tender and the water absorbed.

Stir in the butter and grated pecorino cheese and leave the rice to cool – it will be quicker if you spread it out on a shallow dish. Once cool, mix in the eggs – this is easiest done by hand.

Clear the decks in the kitchen – coating the *arancine* is going to take up all available workspace. Fill three dishes respectively with the flour, beaten eggs and breadcrumbs. Have a bowl of water within easy reach of each hand.

Moisten one hand and scoop up a handful of rice, then flatten it slightly across your palm as if you were making a cup. With the other hand, take a little of the filling and press it into the middle of the rice, adding a cube of the primosale or provolone cheese.

Dip your hand in the water (no, not the one holding the rice and filling), then take some more rice and press it over the filling. Like a potter moulding clay, work and pat the rice together so it forms a ball enclosing the meat and cheese filling. Size can vary from clementine to cannonball, but aim for a manageable 7.5–10cm/3–4in in diameter. The trick is to maximise the ratio of meat filling to rice coating, but as long as it all holds together it doesn't matter too much.

Roll the rice balls in the flour, egg then breadcrumbs and deep-fry. Giovanna, again: 'You can see with your eye when they're cooked!' Drain on kitchen paper and eat hot.

Deep-fried cardoons

Sicilians will fry practically anything that gets within range of the pan. Coatings can be made with breadcrumbs, with flour and eggs or this yeast *pastella* or batter. This recipe uses cardoons, closely related to artichokes, but it's also good for frying pieces of cauliflower, broccoli, aubergines, courgettes... you get the point.

For 4
125g/4oz flour
250ml/8floz water
1 tsp active dried yeast granules
½ tsp oil
1 whole egg, plus 1 egg white
salt
400g/14oz cardoons, trimmed
lemon juice
oil for deep-frying

To make the batter, mix together the flour, water, yeast, oil, whole egg and some salt. Cover and set aside for 1 hour.
Peel off the celery-like strings of the cardoon stalks and cut the flesh into small chunks.
Blanch the cardoons in a saucepan of boiling salted water acidulated with a squeeze of lemon juice. Dry thoroughly with kitchen paper.
Heat some oil for deep-frying. Meanwhile, stiffly whip the egg white and fold it into the batter.
Dip the cardoons in the batter and deep-fry. The batter will puff up, so don't crowd the pan.
Drain and serve sprinkled with sea salt.

Aubergine, pecorino & mint fritters

If the oven is already on, you could roast the aubergines and then scoop out the flesh for a greater depth of flavour, however no prudent Sicilian housewife would heat the oven for this alone.

For 4
4 aubergines, about 900g/2lb in total
125g/4oz currants
300g/10oz breadcrumbs
200g/7oz pecorino cheese, grated
125g/4oz pine nuts, lightly toasted
25g/1oz mint, chopped
salt
peperoncino or black pepper
4 eggs
flour for dusting
oil for deep-frying

Peel and chop the aubergines. Boil for 10 minutes in salted water. They will keep bobbing up to the top of the pan, so give them an occasional push back under the water level with a wooden spoon.
Meanwhile, in a small bowl, soak the currants in a little hot water for 10 minutes, then drain.
Drain the aubergine in a large colander. When it is cool enough to handle, keep it in the colander and squeeze out all the excess liquid you can by hand.
Mix the aubergine pulp with 200g/7oz of the breadcrumbs, plus the cheese, pinenuts, currants, mint, seasonings and 2 of the eggs. The mixture should be soft but not wet. If it seems too firm, add another egg; if it's too squelchy, add more breadcrumbs.
Form the mixture into golf balls, then flatten into discs.
Take 3 plates. Place some flour in one. In another, lightly beat the remaining 2 eggs, and in the third put the remaining 100g/3oz of breadcrumbs. Coat the aubergine discs in flour, egg and breadcrumbs in that order.
Fill a deep-fryer with 7.5–10cm/3–4in of oil and heat gently. When it is shimmering but not smoking, add the aubergine fritters in batches and fry until golden brown on both sides.
Drain on paper towels. Serve hot or at room temperature.

Aubergine, pecorino & mint fritters (above left)

Courgette & mint frittata

Sicilian frittata, a type of omelette, traces its lineage back to the Spanish tortilla. It makes a little go a long way, and can be a thrifty use of leftovers. Fillings may include artichokes, cauliflower, aubergines, fried potatoes, ricotta or simply breadcrumbs. In spring, Sicilians love frittata made with tender young shoots of wild asparagus. Deep-fried mini-frittatas are called *pisci d'ova*, fish shaped like eggs, the ironical comment of those too poor to afford even a plate of fried fish.

For 2

1 tbsp olive oil
½ onion, finely chopped
1 clove garlic, peeled but left whole
1 large courgette, thinly sliced
4 eggs
salt
peperoncino or black pepper
1 tbsp chopped fresh mint
1 tbsp caciocavallo or pecorino cheese, grated

Heat the oil in a 20cm/8in frying pan, preferably nonstick. Gently fry the onion and whole garlic clove until the onion softens but does not brown; the garlic is just to add a subtle hint of flavour.

Keep the heat low, add the courgettes, sprinkle over a little salt and fry for about 10 minutes or until the courgettes have softened but still retain their shape – you can tell it's about right when the seeds seem to swell and become almost translucent.

Lightly beat the eggs with some salt, then add the peperoncino, mint and cheese. Pour into the pan and cook for 10 minutes over a very low heat, occasionally shaking the pan or using a spatula around the edges to make sure the frittata is not sticking. A good nonstick pan makes life a lot easier.

Although the bottom of the frittata should be golden and firm, try not to overcook the centre. Put a plate over the pan, take a deep breath and with a steady hand quickly invert so the frittata slips out upside down, then slide it back into the pan and cook the other side for 5 minutes. Serve warm or at room temperature.

'To eat an egg laid within the hour, bread made the same day, and drink wine from the new harvest can never do you harm.' SICILIAN PROVERB

Loaves and wishes

Bread is fundamental to the Sicilian table, always freshly bought, usually twice a day. A table without bread, they say, is like a day without sunshine. A loaf of *pane rimacinato* made from silky semolina flour with its golden, chewy crumb and dark, crisp crust dotted with sesame seeds, can indeed light up a table, but the saying may also refer to times when a crust was the only alternative to starvation.

The folk memory of such bitter poverty may be fading, but bread remains the staff of life, never to be wasted and surrounded by superstition and religious ritual. An old belief held that anyone who let a crumb fall to the floor would be punished in the afterlife, condemned to sweep it up forever with their eyelashes. Bakers may still cut a cross on each loaf to ward off the evil eye; others will cross themselves before eating a fresh loaf, or never place a loaf upside down on the table. In some small towns, the first ears of ripened wheat are offered to the Madonna, as they once were to Demeter, goddess of grain and abundance.

Reverence and religious ritual merge: plaited Easter breads, for example, have coloured, hard-boiled eggs woven among the braids or are shaped like dolls holding eggs. Tiny white breads in the form of grasshoppers are made for San Biagio in February.

In March, for the Feast of San Giuseppe, it is customary for every community to prepare a banquet or 'altar' at which three needy people represent the Holy Family and are plied with a multitude of dishes and home-baked breads, often fashioned in huge rings called *cucciddatu*. The town of Salemi in western Sicily (declared the capital of Italy for three glorious days after Garibaldi's landing) is renowned for celebratory ornamental breads so intricate they represent animals, saints, flowers, birds, angels and even entire religious scenes. Anna Tasca Lanza, Sicilian food writer and founder of the World of Regaleali cookery school, remembers seeing ex-votos in the form of loaves shaped like body parts, depending on the ailment involved, taken to be blessed on the feast of San Calogero. Carol Field, in *Celebrating Italy*, describes a similar event in Agrigento when bread is thrown at the saint's statue as it parades through the streets.

Sicilian daily bread varies enormously from province to province, town to town, village to village in a seemingly infinite and inventive number of shapes, from crowns and horseshoes to snakes and ladders, even spectacles in homage to Santa Lucia, patron saint of opticians. In Castelvetrano, for example, they still bake a unique black bread, nutty and rich, from a rare local type of wheat called *tumminia*. Outside the most rural areas, however, few people make their own bread anymore; for several centuries, according to American-Sicilian food writer Mary Taylor Simeti, it was actually illegal in

'Put bread to the teeth and hunger resents it.' SICILIAN PROVERB

the Palermo area to bake bread at home because of the municipal monopoly on baking. Bread made from wheat grown on your own land was for the privileged, the grain as valuable as currency. Giuseppe di Lampedusa, author of *The Leopard*, describes a 19th-century farmhouse where a corner of the room was 'bounded by high stiff matting, hiding the honey-coloured wheat taken weekly to the mill for the family's needs'.

In the cities, electric ovens have largely replaced the old brick ones fired with lemon and olive woods that make wonderful, complex sourdough breads, but professional baking still depends on artisan skills rather than mass production techniques – plus, they insist, the special quality of the local water. Everyone remains loyal to their home town versions, invariably declaring, with a sorry shake of the head, when they taste bread from another part of the island, that it is never as good as theirs. How could it be?

Artichoke spread

For 2
300g/10oz artichokes preserved in olive oil, drained
1 small clove garlic
juice of ½ lemon
4 tbsp oil
2 tbsp chopped parsley
2 tbsp chopped mint
salt
peperoncino or black pepper

Blend all the ingredients in a food processor, then leave to mellow for a few hours. Serve on toasted Italian bread.

Caciu all'argintéra

Silversmith's cheese

According to the apocryphal story, this was created by an impoverished silversmith, or his wife, in order that the aroma would give the impression to the neighbours they were rich enough to eat meat. Appearances have always counted for a lot in Sicily.

For 1
olive oil
1 clove garlic
125g/4oz caciocavallo or provolone cheese
1 tbsp red wine vinegar
dried oregano
peperoncino or black pepper
bruschetta (toasted Italian bread)

Heat a little olive oil in a frying pan with the whole, peeled garlic clove. When the garlic colours, remove and discard it.
Cut the cheese into thick slices, and fry quickly until brown. It will shrink and turn lacy round the edges, like a frilly handkerchief, but will cohere and slide onto a spatula or palette knife to be turned over and fried on the other side.
Quickly sprinkle the vinegar over the cheese, allow it to evaporate for a moment, then scatter with oregano and peperoncino or pepper. Serve at once on bruschetta.

Sea view from Sciacca (left), Pani cunzatu (right)

Pani cunzatu

Seasoned Bread

Primrose-coloured Sicilian bread made with semolina flour, hot from the oven, is sometimes sliced crossways, seasoned and doused with generous drizzlings of olive oil, pressed back together and cut into wedges. Fillings can be included and soft rolls can be substituted for whole loaves, but *pani cunzatu*, in its elemental tug at the Sicilian heartstrings, turns a simple sandwich into a philosophy of life.

Slit a fresh sesame or poppy seed roll and fill with sliced caciocavallo or provolone cheese, anchovy fillets, tomatoes, salt, peperoncino or black pepper and oregano.
Drizzle with olive oil and press down firmly. Microwave for 20–30 seconds.

Sfinciuni di Palermo

Pizza Palermo-style

Although often described as deep-dish pizza, this is really a spongy, raised bread with savoury topping. Said to be of Arabic origin, it is, unusually, made with soft wheat flour, baked in large tins and sold by weight. It is still commonly ordered in for parties but these days most young Palermitani would rather go out for pizza.

FOR 1 TRAY, 30.5X43CM/12X17IN

FOR THE DOUGH

1 tsp sugar
150ml/5floz tepid water
1 tsp active dried yeast granules
350g/12oz flour
1 tsp salt
3 tbsp olive oil

FOR THE TOPPING

1 onion, finely sliced
50g/2oz breadcrumbs
100g/4oz caciocavallo or provolone, diced
8 anchovy fillets, chopped
125ml/4floz tomato sauce
1 tbsp dried oregano
peperoncino or black pepper
olive oil

To make the dough, dissolve the sugar in the tepid water. Whisk in the yeast and leave to froth up for 10–15 minutes.
Put the flour and salt in a bowl, make a well in the centre and pour in the yeasty water. Mix well, adding around 125ml/4floz of fresh water extra to make a dough.
Knead for 10 minutes. Add the oil and knead it in thoroughly for another 5 minutes until the dough is elastic-smooth. If the dough seems sticky, flutter a little flour over it; if the dough is very dry, wet your hands with water as you knead.
Form the dough into a ball, place it back in a lightly oiled bowl, cover with plastic wrap and wrap in a towel. Leave for 2–3 hours to rise in a warm draught-free place.
When the dough has expanded 2–3 times in size, punch it down and leave to rise for another 20–30 minutes.
Meanwhile, to make the topping, soften the onion in some olive oil and, in a separate pan, toast the breadcrumbs in some oil.
Oil a baking tray and gently shape the dough to fit the tray. It may resist at first, but be patient and slowly coax out the edges until the surface is flat and even. Oiling your hands may help.
Punch down the dough with your knuckles, then arrange the cheese and anchovies over the top, pressing them into the dough. Scatter over the softened onions and cover with tomato sauce, oregano, the toasted breadcrumbs and some peperoncino.
Drizzle with olive oil, then cover with foil and a kitchen towel and stand in a warm place for 20–30 minutes.
Heat the oven to 220°C/425°F/Gas 7 then bake for 35–40 minutes. Sprinkle with olive oil, cut into squares and serve.

Impanata

Pizza pie

The east and south of Sicily boast a bewildering number of pies and pasties in the shape of Saracen crescents, Swiss rolls, circles and triangles which derive from the Greeks, via the Arabs, out of the Spanish empanadas of the 16th century. Fillings run the gamut from anchovies to *zucca*.

For 4

FOR THE DOUGH

- ½ tsp sugar
- 125ml/4floz tepid water
- 1 tsp active dried yeast granules
- 250g/9oz strong, unbleached white bread flour
- 250g/9oz yellow semolina or durum wheat flour
- 1 tbsp salt
- 4 tbsp olive oil

FOR THE FILLING

- 300g/10oz ruby chard, roughly chopped
- 150g/5oz caciocavallo or provolone cheese, diced
- 150g/5oz ricotta cheese
- 12 sun-dried tomatoes, chopped
- salt
- peperoncino or black pepper
- olive oil

OR

- 1kg/2lb 4oz broccoli florets, lightly steamed
- 250g/9oz tuma or mozzarella cheese, cubed
- 6 anchovies, chopped
- 12 black olives, pitted and chopped
- grated zest of 1 lemon
- 1 tsp dried oregano
- peperoncino or black pepper

Dissolve the sugar in the water, then whisk in the yeast. Leave in a warm place to froth up for 10–15 minutes.

Place the flour and salt in a large bowl, make a well in the centre and pour in the yeasty liquid. Mix together, gradually adding another 250ml/8floz of water or thereabouts until the dough clings together. Work in the olive oil, a little at a time, and knead until the dough is elastic and smooth.

Place in a lightly oiled bowl, cover with plastic wrap, wrap in a towel and leave in a warm place to rise for 2 hours.

Meanwhile, oil and lightly flour a 25cm/10in sandwich tin. In a bowl, combine the ingredients for your chosen filling (except the olive oil) and set aside.

Turn the risen dough onto a lightly floured surface and punch it down, kneading lightly for a few minutes.

Divide the dough into portions of one-third and two-thirds. Roll out the larger portion to make a large, thin circle about 30cm/12in wide, and use it to line the bottom and the sides of the tin – you should have an overhang of about 1cm/½in.

Fill the tin with the chosen filling and drizzle with olive oil.

Roll out the other piece of dough to make a large, thin circle to top the pie. Roll and crimp the overhanging pastry to form as thin and neat a join as you can make and trim off any excess.

Pierce the surface with a fork in several places, then brush the pie with olive oil. Leave to rise for 20-30 minutes.

Heat the oven to 230°C/450°F/Gas 8. Bake the impanata for about 20–30 minutes or until golden. Cool for 10 minutes before removing the pie from the tin.

Alternatively, divide the dough and filling into 6 portions. Roll the dough into circles and place some filling on the lower half of each. Fold over the other half to enclose the filling, pressing the edges firmly together and slightly rolling and crimping the edges of the dough towards the centre to seal the join. It should look like a large Sicilian-Cornish pasty. Leave to rise and bake as above.

Miller of the mountains

Umberto Russo was born to be a miller: the fact that he was an accountant was a mere detail along the road to a greater destiny. All the time he was crunching numbers, he was a man obsessed. As he saw the old mills close, his personal mission became more urgent: to ensure the traditional method of stone-grinding flour was not lost forever. Sicilian tenacity and mule-headed stubbornness kept Umberto fixated despite the bureaucratic problems he encountered: 'I even wrote three times to the President of Italy complaining of the lack of progress in getting a licence.' Did he ever get a reply? 'No, but it made me feel better!'

The renovated Antico Mulino a Pietra, a century-old mill, stands on the outskirts of Longi, a medieval hill town in the Nebrodie National Park. Inside and out, it has been painted the colour of golden wheat; wrought-iron balconies look across ravines to distant towns clinging like barnacles to shipwrecked peaks. The air is intoxicating.

The two immense grinding stones are back in full working order. 'I am still learning,' Umberto explained, 'but it's like a car, you learn to hear if the machine is working well. They were smart in the old days – look how you can turn a ton weight with a single finger! I am enchanted by the simplicity of it all.'

Even more than the grinder, the jolly miller of the mountains is as proud as any new father of his *burratto*, a wooden replica of an ancient machine that further refines the flour. 'It's very simple,' he explained. 'After the wheat is ground, it sieves the flour into different grades of fineness. I personally prefer the bran left in, it's so much better for you, but there's still not much call for it.'

Many traditional varieties of durum wheat, however, have been replaced by high-yield, low-gluten strains as a combined result of farmers abandoning the age-old rotation of crops, poor harvests, low world wheat prices and increasing mechanisation. Attempts are being made to economically sustain the old varieties, but it may be too little, too late. Umberto regrets their passing but still insists, in a crescendo of passion, that Sicilian wheat remains unmatchable. 'You cannot find better. It's a unique product of the sun and rich soil, and is the best in Europe. No, in the *world*!'

Typically, he now supplies bespoke flour to bakers in Milan and Rome, rather than local outlets, as well as grinding organic wheat for wholewheat pasta. 'My hope is that our bakers will return to this flour – we should not save money on the health of our children. Bread is the basis of life, it is sacred.'

Station house, Montallegro

Biscotti al sesamo

Sesame seed biscuits

The name of these popular savoury and yet sweet biscuits varies. Sometimes they are called *biscotti giuggiulena*, after the old-fashioned term for sesame seeds; sometimes *biscotti regina*, queen's biscuits. It's the sort of dispute that can soon engage the passions of partisan Sicilians. Earthy dialect describes them most vividly: *strunzi di ciòcca* and *strunzi d'àncilu*, which mean hen and angel turds respectively.

Makes 20

200g/7oz flour, plus extra for dusting
½ tbsp baking powder
½ tsp salt
100g/3½oz unsalted butter
100g/3½oz sugar
2 eggs
1 tsp vanilla extract or grated lemon zest
125ml/4floz milk
50g/2oz sesame seeds, or fennel seeds

Sift the flour, baking powder and salt together into a large bowl.

In another bowl, beat the butter and sugar together until creamy, then add 1 egg and beat it in well. Repeat with the other egg, then add the vanilla extract or lemon zest.

Gradually stir in the sifted flour; it should combine to make a soft, lightly elastic dough. Form into a ball, dust with flour, cover and leave to rest in the fridge for 30 minutes.

Heat the oven to 200°C/400°F/Gas 6. Put the milk and the sesame or fennel seeds into separate bowls.

Lightly flour a work surface. Divide the rested dough into 20 pieces and shape them into stubby fingers or chipolatas.

Dip each piece of dough in the milk, then coat with the sesame or fennel seeds – you may find the shape becomes easier to mould as you dip each biscuit into the milk.

Bake on a nonstick tray for 20 minutes until light and golden. Be careful not to leave them in the oven any longer, as they have an irritating tendency to turn suddenly from gold to charcoal. The biscuits keep well in an airtight container for about 2 weeks.

Olives & olive oil

In the Valley of the Temples in Agrigento, founded by Greek colonists around 580 BC, there are ancient olive trees, perhaps a thousand years old, whose massive trunks have been sculpted by time into knotted, contorted forms. Stone remains of 5th-century BC olive mills have also been excavated at the ancient colony of Selinunte in the west. The beautiful, bitter olive, embodiment of the sacred and profane, was bequeathed by the Phoenicians and Greeks, who brought the art of grafting the cultivated tree onto the wild oleaster. The Romans took things a step further, efficiently organising the production and distribution of oil on a commercial scale large enough to supply the needs of the Empire.

It seems impossible to imagine Sicilian food in all its colour and brilliance without the olive and its oil, but the Arabs did what they could to wreck the trade. During the Saracen period, they preferred to import their oil, and uprooted many groves to make way for citrus trees. Later, lard became the principal cooking fat until the 18th century, when the Spanish revived production of olive oil, the knowledge kept alive in part by the large religious orders who needed oil for religious use as well as for food, lighting, soap, unguents and medicine.

Sicilian olives include a wonderful variety of single varietals with names you can simply roll round your tongue: *cerasuola, biancolilla* and the perfect Martini olive, *nocellara del Belice*, unusually suited to both table and bottle. Every Sicilian, from marchese to mafioso, is passionate on the subject of olive oil, especially their own. Many city dwellers still get their oil from a few trees on family land or from friends, with the pressing done at a trusted local mill. As Mary Taylor Simeti writes in *On Persephone's Island*, 'It would be unthinkable for anyone to leave his olives at the press and go home until it was time to come and pick up the oil... to ensure that no olives are exchanged or subtracted, nothing added.'

Although Sicily is the third largest olive oil producer in Italy, after Puglia and Calabria, in the past the bulk went for blending and bottling elsewhere. The best oil rarely left the island and Sicilian oil developed a poor reputation. In recent years, however, Sicilian producers have swept the board in international competition with some of the best oils coming from Castelvetrano, near Selinunte, where the silvery green leaves of the *nocellara del Belice* shimmer in the heat against the Olympian sea and sky. There are about a dozen producers in the area, many of whom have won top awards, such as Angela Consiglio who makes organic, cold-pressed Tenuta Rocchetta on her family's estate, as well as Nicolò Peruzza, Girolamo Campagna, Gianfranco Becchina and Agro Verde. A little further afield, U Trappitu and Ravidà are also examples of Sicilian olive oil of outstanding quality and style.

Giovanna Pellegrino's roast peppers

As sold at La Capreria, a bakery-cum-takeaway in Scopello, an exclusive resort high above the sea in western Sicily. La Capreria is also known for its hot *pani cunzatu*.

For 2
- 2 large bell peppers
- 50g/2oz canned tuna in olive oil, drained
- 10–12 green olives, chopped
- 2 tbsp pine nuts, lightly toasted
- peperoncino or black pepper
- lemon juice
- olive oil

Roast the bell peppers, then skin and deseed them and cut the flesh in quarters lengthways.
Mix the tuna, olives, pine nuts and peperoncino with a squeeze of lemon juice.
Place a small spoonful on the pointed end of the sliced pepper.
Roll up like a cigarette and place on a serving dish with the join facing downwards.
Drizzle with olive oil and chill for 1–2 hours before serving.

Olive cunzati

Marinated olives

A traditional Catanian market cry is: 'Marinated olives help the bread slide down and wake up the appetite!' Recipes for this olive salad are legion, but try and use fat green Sicilian table olives such as the *nocellara del Belice*.

For 2–3
- 250g/9oz green olives
- 1 stick celery, thinly sliced
- ½ red onion, finely chopped
- 1 small roasted red or yellow bell pepper, cut into slivers
- ½ small cauliflower, separated into florets
- 1 small carrot, thinly sliced
- 1 tsp red wine vinegar
- 2 tbsp extra virgin olive oil
- peperoncino or black pepper (optional)

Mix all the ingredients together, cover and leave at room temperature for several hours. Stir from time to time. If preferred, leave in the fridge overnight.
Taste and adjust the seasoning (and if necessary bring back to room temperature) before serving.
Alternatively, combine some black olives with orange and lemon peel, whole peeled garlic cloves, fennel seeds, lemon juice and olive oil and marinate as above.

To preserve freshly picked olives, wash them and place in jars with crushed garlic, bay leaves and *salamoia*, a brine solution. After about 2 months, drain, rinse and dress as above.

Cena

Pasta Cosa Nostra

Corleone – the word still strikes a chill. Notorious as a Mafia stronghold, this small mountain town riddled with narrow alleys is almost physically hemmed in by limestone crags and an enormous, riverside boulder topped with a Saracen tower. The town also gave its name to the fictional mob clan in *The Godfather*, but something remarkable has happened here. You could almost call it a miracle. Thanks, perhaps, to San Bernardo, the town's newly consecrated saint, courage has been found to open a Mafia Museum in the heart of the beast. Located in a 400-year-old palace and former orphanage, it is a huge step forward for the town, a potential leap from an age of brutality into one of enlightenment.

My guide, Biagio Salvaggio, President of the Agriculture Commission of Corleone, was a new generation of courageous civic leader, valuing integrity above 'honour'. 'The best way to combat the Mafia,' he insisted, 'is to help young people get on in life, give them hope and show them there's a different way'. Indeed, the day the infamous mafioso Toto Riina was captured, students ran into the streets with a banner proclaiming: 'Finally.'

Walking to the town's dried pasta shop, we even joked that whatever you could say about the Mafia, at least they always ate well. La Corleonese is an atmospheric old shop

The best way to cook pasta? 'You should cook it over a high flame, stir it often and use plenty of water. Pasta should swim in the pan. Everyone knows that.' VITO COLLETTI

with whitewashed walls, marble floor and old wooden fittings overseen by a goodly collection of saints and crucifixes. The wooden shelves were stacked with cellophane packets of 28 different sorts of hand-wrapped pasta, tied with green satin bows. The pasta was made in an adjoining room, the flour mixed with spring water in a large machine with bronze dies. The extruded strands of fresh pasta would be expertly hand-cut, strung over canes in airing cupboards or laid in slatted drawers. After a few blasts of hot air, the pasta is simply dried off naturally for between 40 and 50 hours.

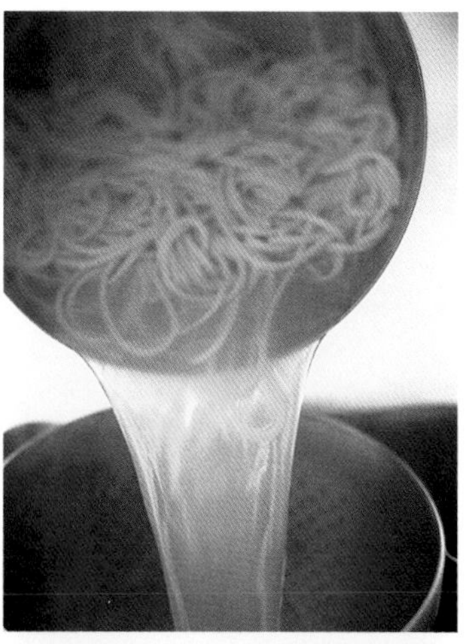

The pasta reflects the colour of the wheat that turns the high, scorched plains around the town into fields of gold. It is a sight unchanged since Sicily was described as the granary of Rome, 'the nurse at whose breast the Roman people are fed', as Roman statesman Cato the Censor wrote. It was left to the Arabs, however, to understand the technology that turned the durum wheat into dried pasta, first recorded on a commercial scale in Trabia, near Palermo, in 1150. One of the oldest known words for pasta is *maccarunne* from the Sicilian *maccare*, meaning to crush the grains to make flour.

WA Paton, a Scots visitor to Palermo in 1898, compared the *maccheroni* hanging out to dry to Japanese curtains: 'along the walls, the streets, in empty gaps, on house tops, from window to window across the narrow streets... where the children play hide and seek amidst the fringes of yellow and white paste'.

Modern times arrived in Corleone in 1840 when the Colletti family opened their shop, catering for the upwardly mobile preference for ready-made pasta. Not much has changed since then – the new machine was acquired in the 1950s and, oh yes, the pasta is now sold over the internet.

Former owner Signor Vito Colletti arrived while I was there, a grizzled pensioner wearing a regulation *coppola*, flat hat. A man of few words, volunteering little until directly questioned, or rather until the words were dragged past the barriers of his lips. What was the secret of good pasta? 'It all depends on the grain. Once we always used russello, a big grain that made the pasta look golden.' A poignant nod of the head. Which pasta was the most traditional? 'In the old days, we preferred bucatini, as the hollow would hold the sugo best.' The expression on his face read: 'You know how it is, no-one understands these things any more...'

What did he think of most pasta today? 'That supermarket stuff – I'd never buy it! You don't know what you're eating.' Another enigmatic wave of the hand. What was the best way to cook pasta? 'You should cook it over a high flame, stir it often and use plenty of water. Pasta should swim in the pan. Everyone knows that.'

Pasta with anchovies & breadcrumbs

In its use of elemental ingredients from the earth and sea, this recipe comes straight from the heart of Sicilian peasant cooking. Anyone who 'licks the anchovy' is said to have fallen on hard times. There are many versions of this popular pasta dish. In Palermo they add chopped tomatoes and oregano; in Catania a nugget of tomato extract. Other recipes include some fried onion or a handful of pine nuts and raisins. This version is from Syracuse, home of the world's first school for professional cooks.

For 2

200g/8oz spaghetti or bucatini
4 tbsp olive oil
2 large cloves garlic, squashed but still whole
100g/4oz breadcrumbs
4 anchovy fillets, chopped
2 tbsp chopped fresh parsley
salt
peperoncino or black pepper

Cook the spaghetti or bucatini according to the packet instructions in a large pan of boiling, salted water.
Meanwhile, heat 3 tbsp of the oil in a frying pan and gently sauté the garlic until the aroma rises up and the cloves begin to colour.
Discard the garlic. Increase the heat a little, add the breadcrumbs and cook, stirring, until they are golden-crisp. Remove them from the pan with a slotted spoon and set aside.
Add 1 tbsp of oil to the pan and cook the anchovies over a low heat until they start to dissolve.
Return the breadcrumbs to the pan, stir in the parsley and check the seasoning.
Drain the pasta, but reserve a little cooking water to add in case the crumb and anchovy sauce seems very dry.
Toss the sauce and pasta together and serve.

Spaghetti with peas, pancetta & mint

The Sicilian imagination has no limits when it comes to pasta shapes. Reciting them is like counting rosary beads: rings, ruffles, ribbons, bows, spirals, shells, ridged or smooth, flat as a ruler or stiletto-sharp… but spaghetti remains *numero uno*. This is a popular everyday family recipe.

For 2

200g/8oz spaghetti
1 tbsp olive oil
2 cloves garlic, peeled
100g/4oz peas, defrosted if frozen
50g/2oz pancetta, cubed
peperoncino or black pepper
4 tbsp chopped fresh mint
4 tbsp grated pecorino or parmesan cheese, or mollica (toasted breadcrumbs)

Bring a large pot of salted water to the boil and cook the spaghetti according to the packet instructions.
Heat the oil in a frying pan over medium heat. Add the whole garlic cloves and remove when toasty-brown on both sides.
Add the pancetta, fry for a few minutes, then add the peas. Take care if using defrosted frozen peas as the oil may spit alarmingly when the peas hit the pan.
Add the peperoncino or black pepper and fry gently for several minutes until the pasta is ready.
When the pasta is cooked and the pancetta crispy, toss it all together with the mint and add the cheese, or sprinkle with mollica.

'If the pot doesn't boil, don't throw in the pasta.' SICILIAN PROVERB

Spaghetti with peas, pancetta & mint (right)

Pasta con le sarde

Pasta with sardines

The story goes that when Euphemius of Messina returned from exile in Tunisia to mount a military expedition in 827, his Arab cooks, on landing at the harbour of Mazara, ingeniously put together the first ingredients that came to hand: wild fennel, currants, saffron and pine nuts and, of course, the freshest of sardines. This is another recipe from Linda Ruggiero.

For 8

1 large bunch wild fennel leaves, chopped, or the tops of fennel bulbs, or the leaves of garden fennel
olive oil
1kg/2lb4oz fresh sardines, headed and filleted
6 shallots, finely chopped
4 anchovies
2 tbsp 'strattu or 4 tbsp tomato paste
150ml/5floz white wine
150ml/5floz water
2 tbsp currants
2 tbsp pine nuts
2 pinches saffron strands, soaked in a little warm water
1kg/2lb4oz bucatini
mollica (toasted breadcrumbs)

Put the fennel leaves in a large pan of water, bring to the boil and simmer for 20 minutes.
Meanwhile heat 8 tbsp of olive oil in a saucepan and gently sauté the shallots, then add the anchovies and stir until dissolved
Add half the fresh sardines, the 'strattu or tomato paste, wine and water. Stir for a few minutes, then add the currants and pine nuts. Leave to cook for 15 minutes over a low heat.
Drain the fennel leaves, reserving the water.
Heat a little more oil in a frying pan. Add the fennel and sauté over a high heat for a few minutes, breaking the leaves up with a spoon.
Add the fennel and 3 ladles of the reserved cooking water to the sardine mixture. Stir in the saffron and, if the mixture seems very thick, some more water. Cook over a low heat for 10 minutes.
Stir in the rest of the sardines and cook for another 10 minutes.
Bring the rest of the reserved cooking water to the boil, add some salt and the pasta. Cook according to the packet instructions.
Drain the pasta and serve with the sardine sauce, sprinkled with toasted breadcrumbs.

Mondello (left)

Spaghetti with prawns picchi-pacchi

Picchi-pacchi means a lightly cooked, fresh tomato sauce – quite how it got its lip-smacking name, no one seems to know, though one explanation is that it mimics the sound of the wooden spoon breaking up the tomato in the pan. The sauce is commonly found throughout Sicily; in the west they use garlic and no onion, in the east onion, but no garlic. This recipe comes from Agrigento in the south, where they use both garlic and onion.

For 2

1 medium onion, finely chopped
4 tbsp olive oil
200g/8oz ripe tomatoes, peeled, seeded and chopped
1 large clove garlic, finely chopped
salt
200g/8oz spaghetti
300g/12oz prawns, shelled
white wine
fresh parsley, chopped

In a frying pan, heat the oil and sauté the onion gently until it is soft and translucent but not brown.
Add the tomatoes and garlic and cook for 10 minutes, crushing the tomatoes with a wooden spoon until they start to go limp, then add salt to taste.
Cook the spaghetti according to the packet instructions in plenty of boiling, salted water.
Add the prawns to the tomato sauce and simmer for 5 minutes.
Sprinkle a little white wine into the sauce. Turn up the heat and cook a few minutes to burn off the alcohol, then reduce the heat and simmer the sauce a few minutes more.
Add plenty of parsley – you always need more than you think.
Drain the spaghetti and toss with the prawn sauce. Serve *subito!*

La bottarga di Favignana

'As bottarga becomes increasingly fashionable, its old description as the caviar of the poor no longer seems accurate.'

Favignana rose up ahead of us, a smudge of land like a thumbprint between the sky and the sea. The hydrofoil skipped the short stretch of aquamarine water across to the butterfly-shaped island fluttering off the western coast of Sicily. A Saracen castle sits atop the mountain ridge that bisects the largest of the Egadi Isles, but their history goes back much further. It was here on Favignana that Odysseus was shipwrecked and his men turned into swine by Circe; here that the treaty to end the First Punic War was signed; and here that the sands of time are now running out for the ancient, bloody but heroic tuna fishing ritual known as *la mattanza*.

Alessandro Sammartano is the sole remaining artisan producer of bottarga, preserved tuna roe, on Favignana. The technique of preserving tuna roe dates back to the Byzantines, and Alessandro had learnt the art from his father-in-law after the latter lost his job when the Florio tuna works closed. Most Italian bottarga now comes from imported fish, and even the Favignana tuna has to be processed across the water in Trapani. The whole egg sacs must be skilfully removed as soon as the tuna is caught, before the fish are packed onto fast container ships that will ferry them to Tokyo's insatiable sushi bars.

As soon as Alessandro receives the precious eggs, they are cleaned then brined. Over the next few weeks they are washed, salted and massaged several times by hand to stretch them into their characteristic torpedo shape and eliminate air pockets. The bottarga is pressed each time between wooden planks like double-decker sandwich fillings, the top board weighted down by marble blocks. Until recently, the weights were made from the local stone, tufa, hewn out of the largely abandoned quarries that have been transformed into spectacular, wild sunken gardens clad with wild thyme and capers. Finally, the bottarga is rinsed and sun-dried for up to two months so that it becomes dark red and highly compressed. Each evening the boards are brought back under cover, painstaking and skillful work. Too little or too much salt and the bottarga will be ruined, too long in the sun and it dries up.

As bottarga becomes increasingly fashionable, its old description as the caviar of the poor no longer seems accurate. Alessandro, however, is still pessimistic about tuna stocks: 'I doubt we will see the great shoals again, the waters have been so badly fished and polluted. International action is needed to conserve stocks, and now that the *mattanza*, the way the tuna has traditionally been killed, has become a tourist attraction it has brought protesters who do not understand its history and true nature. The future for this traditional way of life is in jeopardy. It makes me very sad.'

Pasta with bottarga

According to Alessandro Sammartano, serving bottarga with pasta is a modern idea. The traditional way to eat bottarga is simply like salami, with bread and tomatoes. 'In the old days, we just ate the things we had at hand. We never had pigs on Favignana, so we ate the tuna instead.' Be as generous with the parsley as you are meagre with the bottarga.

For 2

15–25g/½–1oz bottarga, shaved into flakes
olive oil
200g/ 8oz bucatini
1 small clove garlic, finely chopped
fresh parsley, chopped
1 fresh red chilli pepper, finely chopped (optional)
fresh basil

Soften the flakes of bottarga in a little olive oil.
Cook the pasta according to the packet instructions in plenty of boiling salted water.
Gently heat the garlic and parsley in 3–4 tbsp of olive oil.
Quickly stir in the chilli pepper and the bottarga – this takes seconds, not minutes.
Drain the pasta and mix with the bottarga sauce.
Top with shredded basil leaves.

Pasta alla Etna

Volcanic Pasta

For 4
400g/14oz squid ink spaghetti, or squid ink rice
400ml/14floz tomato sauce, well seasoned with peperoncino
primosale, provolone or mozzarella cheese, thinly sliced

Cook the pasta or rice in plenty of boiling, salted water, according to the packet instructions. Meanwhile, heat the tomato sauce in a separate saucepan.
Drain the pasta or rice and pile on a serving platter so it resembles black Mount Etna.
Flatten the top of the pasta or rice slightly and cover with thin slices of cheese (to represent snow).
Complete the spectacular effect by drizzling a little bubbling, fiery tomato sauce over the summit and serve the rest in a jug alongside.

Pasta alla Stromboli

Not to be outdone, the Aeolian Islands in the north-east have their own volcanic version.

For 4
400g/14oz spaghetti
1 onion, finely chopped
1 clove garlic, finely chopped
olive oil
500g/1lb cherry tomatoes, halved
salt
peperoncino
175g/6oz ricotta salata, crumbled

Cook the pasta in plenty of boiling, salted water, according to the packet instructions.
Meanwhile, in a frying pan, lightly fry the onion and garlic in oil. Add the tomatoes and cook for a few minutes, seasoning well (to represent the heat of the volcano).
Drain the pasta and pile on a serving platter.
Top with the tomato sauce, then the cheese (to symbolise ash).

Views of Mount Etna (left)

Spaghetti with tuna, caper & mint sauce

Another recipe from the Aeolian Islands.

For 4
100g/4oz capers
220g/8oz canned tuna in oil
25g/1oz fresh mint
juice of ½ lemon
150ml/5floz extra virgin olive oil
salt
400g/14oz spaghetti
peperoncino or black pepper

Whizz the capers, tuna and mint in a blender with a drop of water.
Turn into a bowl and add the lemon juice and enough of the olive oil to make a moist sauce. Add salt to taste.
Cook the spaghetti according to the packet instructions, then drain and mix with the tuna sauce.
Sprinkle with peperoncino or black pepper to give a little kick.

'Stirred-up' pasta and cauliflower

Pasta and cauliflower is a popular combination throughout Sicily. This version comes from Palermo, but recipes vary. In Enna, they add tomato sauce and grated cheese, while Trapani has a complex baked version enriched with pork *ragù*, cheese, toasted almonds and hard-boiled eggs.

For 2
½ cauliflower, florets only
1 slice lemon
1 bay leaf
25g/1oz currants
2 tbsp olive oil
½ medium onion, finely chopped
3–4 anchovy fillets
25g/1oz pine nuts
1 tsp saffron strands, soaked in a little hot water
200g/8oz bucatini or penne
fresh parsley, chopped
mollica (toasted breadcrumbs)

Put a large pan of salted water on to boil. Add the cauliflower, lemon and bay leaf and cook for 10–15 minutes until soft – we are not talking *al dente* here.
Meanwhile soak the currants in hot water for 10 minutes.
Heat the olive oil in a frying pan. Add the onion and soften slowly over a low heat.
When the onion is cooked but only just beginning to brown, add the anchovies, torn into small pieces. Use a wooden spoon to break them up further. Stir them around in the pan so that they meld into the oil and onions.
Stir in the pine nuts and, when they're nice and oily, add the drained currants. Let them cook for a few minutes, while you drain the cauliflower, reserving the liquid. Discard the bay and lemon.
Add the saffron, cauliflower and a ladle of the cooking liquid to the sauce. Swish it all together – it needs to be quite moist, so add more cooking water if necessary.
Start to squash the cauliflower with the back of a wooden spoon. Let it cook gently for about 15 minutes, mashing down the cauliflower to a soft porridge consistency as if you were making baby food. It doesn't look appetising, but have faith in the flavour.
Reheat the cauliflower cooking water to cook the pasta. Add some fresh water if there isn't enough. Cook the pasta according to the packet instructions.
Drain and toss with the cauliflower sauce. Sprinkle with lots of parsley and toasted breadcrumbs before serving.

Pasta alla Norma

There are numerous versions of this homage to music and food, based on variations on a theme of pasta, aubergines, tomatoes and ricotta salata. The composer Bellini was born in Catania, and according to legend, on the opening night in 1890 of both the city's jewel of an opera house and his opera *Norma,* the public were so overwhelmed, they insisted on marking the occasion by naming a dish after the event. Another story attributes the name to the compliment paid to a Catanese cook by a famous Sicilian actor in the 1920s who declared, with typical hyperbole, that his meal had been 'as good as Norma!'. A more prosaic explanation, however, is that *norma* in Sicilian dialect means 'rule' or 'standard' – in other words, pasta made with ingredients that are the staples of the Catanian diet. Without the cheese – and with the aubergine cut into cubes – this dish sometimes goes by the less musical name of Pasta with Cockroaches.

For 2
1 large aubergine, cut into sticks about the size of french fries
salt
olive oil
250ml/9floz tomato sauce
200g/8oz spaghetti or penne
100g/4oz ricotta salata, or feta cheese
fresh basil
peperoncino or black pepper

Salt the aubergine sticks generously and leave them in a colander for 1 hour to extract the bitter juices.
Wash the aubergine thoroughly and pat dry with a clean towel.
Heat 1cm/½in of olive oil in a large frying pan. Fry the aubergine sticks over medium heat until golden brown. Blot thoroughly with kitchen paper and set aside.
Cook the pasta according to the packet instructions in a large saucepan with plenty of boiling, salted water.
Heat the tomato sauce, then mix with the drained pasta, half the cheese and the basil.
Arrange the aubergine sticks on the top and scatter with the remaining cheese. Serve while humming *Casta Diva*. Or maybe not.

Pasta alla Norma (right)

Fennel seed sausage & scrambled eggs

It's a rare Sicilian who will buy sausages without standing in front of the butcher ensuring they are made to personal specifications. Carlo Middione gives a recipe in *The Food of Southern Italy*, and explains they were once described as *al punto del coltello* – hacked sausage – because 'the meat was painstakingly cut into little bits, allowing all of the spices and flavouring to penetrate it on all surfaces'. A popular way of cooking them is in a skewered coil on the char-grill (*alla bracie*), or fried with bitter wild greens.

Sicilian sausages are thin and made from coarsely chopped pork and wild fennel seeds. Some prefer a combination of pork and veal, others a mixture flavoured with cheese and white wine. Opinions vary on whether the cheese should be grated or cubed, and there are those who leave it out altogether but add parsley. The mixture should not be too fatty, or too lean; it should be just right. So, the only way to ensure you don't end up with someone else's inferior recipe is to stand and watch the butcher make them.

For 2

1 medium onion, sliced
olive oil
2–3 fennel seed sausages, chopped, casing removed if thick
4 eggs
25g/1oz pecorino cheese, grated
salt
peperoncino or black pepper
toasted Italian bread

Fry the onion slowly in olive oil until soft and golden.
Add the sausage and fry for 10 minutes.
Beat the eggs, then mix in the cheese, salt and peperoncino.
Pour the egg mixture over the sausagemeat and scramble gently.
Serve over slices of toasted bread.

Grilled sausage coil (above),
View from Cianciana towards Sciacca (left)

'It's a rare Sicilian who will buy sausages without standing in front of the butcher ensuring they are made to personal specifications.'

The lentils of Ustica

The rare brick and slate lentils look like Lilliputian versions of pebbles on the seashore of Ustica. The island, the summit of a large submerged volcano, was inhabited in prehistoric and Roman times but then abandoned until the 18th century, when the Bourbons brought families over from the Aeolian Islands to cultivate the land. The islanders live in houses painted with fanciful murals, and try to make a living from vines, figs, prickly pears, wheat and other cereals, especially lentils, and from tourists attracted by the transparent waters of the National Marine Park.

The Usticesi are fiercely proud of the tiny lentils which have always played an important part in the frugal island diet, particularly in stews and soups scented with basil and wild fennel. The lentils of Ustica need no prior soaking and have a short cooking time, keeping their shape and flavour intact where lesser lentils either turn to mush or harden unpleasantly.

Nicola Longo, one of only three producers left, has written a scholarly and witty account of how the lentils were once shipped to Naples and Palermo in a 'golden age of lentils' that flourished until post-war years. An unsolicited 19th-century testimonial from the Archduke Louis Hapsburg praised them as 'extremely small but extremely tasty'. The late 1970s, however saw a huge decline in production: 'The general economic crisis, the emigration of young people and the first stirrings of tourism, signalled the beginning of the end for our old and dignified local ways of farming that were no longer competitive.' Exports stopped and the lentils became a niche product for local consumption and tourist souvenirs. Yet Signor Longo's outlook is positive – he sees the potential for their discovery by the rest of the world.

The lentils are still cultivated entirely by hand, the ploughs pulled by donkey-power, and as Signor Longo drily comments: 'The time for planting the seeds is still frequently the subject of deep and fierce debate in the barbershop amongst the waiting clients.'

In June the plants are harvested, tied into sheaves and left to dry in the field; they are then gathered into large oilskin cloths with a piece of rope at each corner, and knotted like a large handkerchief. In the threshing room, the plants are crushed between discs of lavic rock, once turned by two cows, now by motor. The husks are then tossed with a wooden pitchfork, resulting in the gradual accumulation of two satisfying piles of debris and lentils.

'At this point,' continues Signor Longo, 'the grader enters the scene... they used to be legendary characters, possessing a skill that was only granted to the most elect.' The grading is traditionally done with a hide sieve, hung from three wooden poles, and finally the lentils are bagged 'along with their inseparable companions, the tiny stones the housewife must always carefully remove before cooking'.

Maccu di San Giuseppe

Served on St Joseph's Day, this mixed bean soup (like all bean soups) improves in flavour if left overnight.

For 6

150g/6oz dried, skinned broad beans or butter beans
100g/4oz dried peas
50g/2oz chickpeas
50g/2oz dried haricot or cannellini beans
50g/2oz Italian lentils
1 onion, chopped
2 handfuls borage leaves, or spinach or chard
1 handful wild fennel leaves, or the tops of cultivated or garden fennel
15g/½oz fennel seeds
350g/12oz canned tomatoes
salt
peperoncino or black pepper
extra virgin olive oil

Soak all the pulses, except the lentils, overnight.

Next day, drain, rinse and place all the soaked pulses in a large pan with the lentils. Cover with water and bring to the boil. Cover and simmer for 1–2 hours or until tender.

Add the onion, greens, seeds, tomatoes and season to taste with salt. Cook for another hour or so until all the pulses are soft, adding more liquid, if necessary.

Season with plenty of peperoncino or black pepper and drizzle some olive oil over each bowl before serving.

Lentil soup

Tradition holds that prosperity is ensured for the year ahead if you eat lentils on New Year's Eve. No lentils, no money – so why take the risk? To improve the chance of good fortune, the next day you should also eat macaroni, bearing in mind the Sicilian proverb: 'He who eats macaroni on New Year's Day, for the whole of the year keeps trouble away.'

For 4

200g/7oz Italian lentils
2.5 litres/4 pints water
225g/8oz canned, chopped tomatoes
2 sticks celery, chopped, plus some celery leaves
1 onion, finely chopped
25g/1oz fresh mint or basil, chopped
100g/3½oz small pasta
salt
peperoncino or black pepper
extra virgin olive oil

Put the lentils, water, vegetables and half the herbs in a large saucepan and slowly bring to the boil.

Simmer, stirring occasionally, for 40 minutes or until the lentils are cooked.

Season the soup to taste and add the pasta. Simmer for a further 5 minutes or until the pasta is cooked.

Serve the soup in bowls sprinkled with the rest of the mint or basil and a trickle of olive oil.

LACOSTE
ue
i mare
2 - VIA LICATA, 295

Caponata with San Bernardo sauce

An intriguing sweet-sour recipe from the private family archives of Giuliana Spadaro di Passanitello, who comments that '*La caponata*, an ancient recipe of Latin origin, was a seafood dish invented by fishermen. Over time, the seafood was lost and only the vegetables remained.' She is one of three founders of L'Olmo, a cookery school based in the enchanting lava-stone home of Marina Paternò Castello di San Giuliano, near Taormina.

For 6

100g/4oz Italian bread, diced
olive oil
50g/2oz toasted almonds
2 large anchovy fillets
juice of 1 orange
1 tsp unsweetened cocoa
½ tbsp sugar
225ml/8floz white wine vinegar
225ml/8floz water
4 aubergines
1kg/2lb4oz small whole squid
flour
orange slices and finely chopped, toasted almonds

Fry the bread in olive oil until golden. Drain on kitchen paper.
Place in a mortar with the toasted almonds and pound to the consistency of breadcrumbs, or grind coarsely in a food processor.
Add the anchovies and orange juice and mix to a smooth paste.
Pour the mixture into a saucepan and add the cocoa, sugar, vinegar and water. Place over a very gentle heat and cook, stirring often.
As the sauce thickens, slowly bring it up to boiling point, then remove from the heat and set aside to cool. Adjust the balance of flavours as desired and leave for several hours or overnight.
Cut the aubergine into quarters, or into halves and then thirds, depending on the size. Soak in salted water for at least 1 hour.
Dry well, then dust with flour and sauté in olive oil until golden. Drain on kitchen paper and set aside.
Dust the squid with flour, deep-fry in olive oil, then drain on kitchen paper.
Arrange the aubergine on a serving dish, cover with a little of the sauce, and arrange the squid around the edge. Decorate with sliced oranges and finely chopped, toasted almonds.

Evening in Sciacca (left)

Caponata di Eleonora Consoli

Caponata is best made 2–3 days in advance of eating to give the flavours time to mellow. This recipe comes from Eleonora Consoli, a distinguished writer who also runs a cookery school at her beautifully restored country house in Viagrande, Catania. It typifies the way in which Sicilian cooking can begin with one plain, homespun ingredient and end up in a state of voluptuous abandonment. Use round purple Tunisian aubergines, if possible, rather than the elongated dark ones.

For 4

4 aubergines, cubed
2 sticks celery, sliced into 5cm/2in pieces
600ml/1 pint olive oil
4 bell peppers, deseeded and sliced
1 onion, sliced
1 salted anchovy, or 2 fillets in oil
3 tbsp tomato paste
2 tbsp capers
100g/4oz green olives, stoned
2 tbsp sultanas or currants
150ml/5floz white wine vinegar
4 tbsp sugar
salt
black pepper
toasted almonds, basil, mint (optional)

Salt the aubergine generously and leave to drain in a colander for 1 hour to extract the bitter juices. Rinse well and pat dry.
Cook the celery for 10–15 minutes in a pan of salted, boiling water. Drain well and pat dry.
Heat 150ml/5floz of the olive oil and fry the celery over a medium heat until it is just crunchy. Drain on kitchen paper.
Top up the oil if necessary and fry the peppers over medium heat until they start to soften but are still crisp. Drain on kitchen paper.
Add more oil and fry the aubergines over a high heat until they are cooked but still keep their shape. Drain well on kitchen paper.
In the remaining oil, fry the onion over a medium heat until golden, taking care that it does not brown.
Reduce the heat, add the anchovy and cook until it breaks down. Stir in the tomato paste.
Add the cooked celery, bell peppers and aubergine to the onion mixture, followed by the capers, olives, sultanas, vinegar, sugar, salt and pepper. Cook, stirring, over a high heat for a few minutes.
Serve hot or cold, with a sprinkling of mint or basil and some chopped toasted almonds. The caponata will keep for up to 1 month in the fridge stored in an airtight container.

Sagra di Carciofi

'Don't peel the outer leaves, or the heart will burn inside, and keep drizzling olive oil to keep them moist.'

An effigy of a giant, slender artichoke, flushed purple, mauve and green, stands proudly, if somewhat surreally, in the main piazza of Cerda, near Palermo. This is Artichokeville, the town of artichokes, dedicated to the cultivation and eating of *Cynara scolymus*. The season lasts from mid-November to April, culminating in a festival, *Sagra di Carciofi,* with barbecued artichokes and artichoke risotto for all-comers. The town's restaurants vie to present a 'choke-with-every-course menu, but the First Family of artichokes is undoubtedly the Nasca clan, owners of two fine restaurants and a bar.

At Nasca 2, a no-frills trattoria with a view of the mountains and fields filled with endless rows of artichokes, the walls are decorated with themed paintings, including an eye-catching one of phosphorescent artichokes glowing in the moonlight in front of the Chiesa Madre. There was no choice, simply an array of little dishes that covered the entire surface of the table – artichokes stewed in oil and vinegar, braised with tomato and garlic or with lemon and oil, whole roasted artichokes the size of oranges, artichoke frittata, deep-fried artichokes, caponata made with artichokes, grilled artichokes, raw baby artichoke salad dressed with oil, lemon, peperoncino and breadcrumbs, home-made *casareccia* (a short, twisted pasta) with artichoke and wild fennel sauce.

At weekends, Cerda is packed with people in search of artichokes. As my travelling companion Rosy, ever pragmatic, said: 'All Palermo comes here on Sundays – where else can you eat so much food for so little money?'

There were other pasta sauces, grilled meats and fennel seed sausages, but they seemed incidental to the main business of the meal. Artichoke mania was in the air; the elegant matron at the next table leant over to discuss artichoke recipes. She liked to fry them in sections with an egg-and-breadcrumb coating, or sometimes with a yeast batter; that is when she wasn't cooking them stuffed with breadcrumbs, garlic and anchovies, stewed in water and oil. At the end of the season, boiled artichokes were eaten at the end of a meal. Artichokes, everyone agreed, are good for you, full of iron and other healthy things. Drinking the water in which they are cooked, I was advised, flushed out the urinary system a treat.

Artichokes are the cultivated form of the wild cardoon, a plant of either North African or Sicilian origin that was known to the Greeks and Romans. The Cerda artichokes are svelte and delicately tinted, small and tender enough to eat whole apart from a few outer leaves, and quite unlike the jolly green globes of more northern lands. In season, they're sold from street barrows, their serrated leaves and lanky stems piled high. The question of thorns though is, well, a thorny one, and opinions vary across the

island. Signor Nasca said they only use locally-grown *spinosi di Palermo*, which he insisted are superior in taste, at his restaurants. The variety needs careful handling, but he regrets the increasing cultivation of thorn-free artichokes: 'Modern women don't want to risk getting thorns in their hand!'

What was his favourite way of cooking artichokes? 'I like to sauté them over high heat in a covered pan with oil, butter, onions, wild fennel and broth,' he replied. 'And don't turn them with a wooden spoon; just keep shaking the pan. For a pasta sauce I just add bay leaves and ricotta. But the simpler you cook them, the better.'

Over *cannoli* and artichoke liqueur, Rosy described how it was an essential part of the festivities on *Pasquetta* (Easter Monday) to roast artichokes either directly on hot embers or by chargrilling them in a special home-made grid. The artichokes are pounded on the ground to loosen the leaves, then stuffed with mint, parsley, garlic and sea salt: 'Don't peel the outer leaves, or the heart will burn inside,' she advised, 'and keep drizzling olive oil to keep them moist.' Then in typically discouraging but accurate Sicilian fashion she added: 'but, really, you have to be an expert to do it right.'

Artichoke caponata

An all-white version of this dish, 'rabbit' *caponata*, is made in Pollizi Generosa at Christmas with cardoons and potatoes, but not tomatoes. The name is ironic, as chef, artist and historian Santo Lipani of L'Orto dei Cappuccini explained. Many were too poor to even afford rabbit. It can be difficult to find the right sort of artichokes for this recipe – the globular ones simply won't do. If you can't find good small ones it is best to simply admit defeat and substitute a good brand of jarred artichokes in olive oil.

For 4–6

12 small fresh artichokes, or artichokes in oil
½ lemon, plus a squeeze of lemon juice
1 large onion, finely chopped
4 tbsp olive oil
500g/1lb tomatoes, skinned, deseeded and chopped
100g/4oz capers
100g/4oz green olives
2 sticks celery, chopped
4 tbsp sugar
4 tbsp white wine vinegar
salt
orange and lemon slices

To trim fresh artichokes, cut off the stem, remove the outer leaves, trim the top and cut in half. If the artichoke has a developed, prickly choke, remove it with a sharp knife.
Rub the fresh artichokes with the lemon half, then drop into a bowl of water mixed with a little lemon juice.
In a large pan, fry the onion in some olive oil until it starts to soften. Add the chopped tomatoes, capers, olives and celery and cook gently for 10 minutes.
Drain the fresh artichokes and add them to the mixture. If you are using jarred artichokes preserved in oil, drain them and add to the pan at this point. Cook for 5 minutes
Season the mixture with sugar, vinegar and salt, then cover and cook for another 10–15 minutes until the artichokes are tender.
Cool and leave the caponata to stand a few hours or overnight before serving it decorated with slices of orange and lemon.

Sweet & sour pumpkin (left)

La frittedda

For 4–6

6 small artichokes
juice of ½ lemon
4 shallots, chopped
4–5 tbsp olive oil
175g/6oz very young broad beans (shelled weight)
175g/6oz fresh peas (shelled weight)
salt
lardo or bread triangles fried in olive oil (optional)
2 tbsp vinegar (optional)
1 tsp sugar (optional)

Remove the spiky parts and tough outer leaves of the artichokes, and cut off the stalk and the top. Cut into halves or quarters, depending on the size, remove any prickly choke and immerse in a bowl of water mixed with lemon juice.
Lightly fry the shallots in olive oil, then add the artichokes, broad beans, peas and some salt. Moisten with a little water, cover and cook gently for about 20 minutes, stirring from time to time. Add a splash of water if it seems to be drying out.
Serve with pieces of lardo, if wished, or fried bread. Alternatively, add the vinegar and sugar, then cool and chill before serving.

Sweet & sour pumpkin

For 4

4 tbsp olive oil
4 garlic cloves, peeled
1kg/2lb4oz pumpkin, or 2 butternut squash, peeled, deseeded and sliced
4 tbsp white wine vinegar
50g/2oz sugar
¼ tsp ground cinnamon
a handful of mint leaves, roughly chopped
salt
peperoncino or black pepper

Heat the olive oil with the garlic cloves in a large frying pan.
Add the pumpkin and cook until it chars around the edges, tossing and turning frequently.
Remove the pumpkin from the pan with a slotted spoon and arrange it in a serving dish. Discard the garlic.
Sprinkle the vinegar, sugar, cinnamon, mint and some salt and peperoncino or black pepper into the pan. Cook over a medium heat for 1–2 minutes, the pour over the pumpkin.
Leave to cool, then cover and chill for several hours before serving.

Mountain cheese & ricotta

High in the mountains above Cinisi, the streams flow pure and clear. Manna from the flowering ash is still used here for medicinal purposes, and they make ricotta and cheese in a setting and with a method that has scarcely changed over the centuries. Once the people who lived here were well off, the proud owners of sheep, cows and olives; those who lived by the sea were the poor ones. Now any land along the coast is highly valuable, while much of the interior is deserted and abandoned.

Joseph Maniaci is a *vaccaro*, one of a vanishing breed of cowmen and cheesemakers. He knows he is the last of the line, and laments, 'Nothing can replicate the mountain air, the smoke from the olive wood and all the good dirt! The pressures are closing in. Eventually they'll make us close.'

There are still about half a dozen cheesemakers left in the village, each with their own herd of long-horned black cows. They share out the milk, but when Joseph tried to start a marketing co-operative no-one was interested. 'It would have been far better economically for us all,' he said. 'I've always had a passion for cheesemaking. My brothers and sisters went to school but I just wanted to make cheese. My children never want to come up here, but it's part of my heritage. I love what I do and I'm proud of it.'

The cheese and ricotta – 'Ricotta is not cheese, ricotta is ricotta!' – is made in a tiny stone hut that you could mistake for a heap of rubble. The heat was fierce as we entered; my eyes stung with smoke. The walls were blackened, ancient wooden tubs crowded the packed earth floor, and a copper cauldron was held in place by a rough stone grate. The cheeses are shaped and matured in a second room with thick stone walls to provide natural air conditioning.

As Joseph talked, he stirred the milk until it began to boil and separate. When he threw more olive wood onto the fire, flames spurted out, covering him in sparks and ashes. Every day he came to the high pasture to make ricotta and caciocavallo, once or twice a day depending on the season. He checks the temperature with a thermometer now, but 'in the old days you stuck in your hand, and when you couldn't stand the heat you knew it was time to add more milk'.

The work is physically demanding: from turning and folding the *pasta filata* (stretched curd) with a pole so it clings together in a smooth, undulating mass, to kneading a steaming white pillow of paste submerged in a low tub on the ground. At one point he produced a fierce-looking sickle, tilted a barrel of coagulating curds and almost disappeared inside as he hauled out each triangular, dripping chunk, but he talked to the cheese as tenderly as if it were a woman.

Joseph ladled out a warm clump of curds, wet with whey. A bowl of warm ricotta is still one of the greatest gestures of hospitality a Sicilian can offer the visitor. Creamy and slippery, with a comforting lactic aroma, it was like eating little white clouds.

'Galatea, why do you treat your lover harshly? You are whiter than ricotta, gentler than a lamb, livelier than a calf, firmer than an unripe grape...'

THEOCRITUS

Ricotta-stuffed bell peppers

FOR 4
olive oil
4 large bell peppers, mixed or single colours
4 shallots, finely chopped
1 clove garlic, finely chopped
5–6 anchovy fillets, chopped
peperoncino or black pepper
50g/2oz black olives
500g/1lb2oz ricotta
2 tomatoes, peeled, deseeded and chopped
3 tbsp capers
fresh basil leaves, shredded

Preheat the oven to 200°C/400°F/Gas mark 6. Oil a baking dish in which the bell peppers will neatly fit upright.

Slice the tops off the bell peppers and reserve. Scrape out all the seeds and pith, then set the bell peppers aside.

Gently fry the shallot, garlic, anchovy fillets and peperoncino together in a little olive oil for a few minutes until the anchovies melt. Set aside to cool.

Stone and chop the olives, then mix with the ricotta, tomatoes, capers and basil. Combine this with the shallot mixture.

Stuff the bell peppers and top with their little 'hats'.

Drizzle well with olive oil and bake for 30 minutes or until the bell peppers start to wrinkle and blister. Serve hot or cold.

Basics

Tomato sauce

Sicilians always put sugar in their tomato sauce. The longer it simmers, the more it concentrates and intensifies the flavour.

Makes about 600ml/1 pint

450g/1lb fresh tomatoes, or 800g/28oz canned tomatoes
1 small onion, chopped
1 clove garlic (optional)
2 tbsp olive oil
several basil leaves, roughly shredded
1 tsp sugar
salt

Slice off the stalk of the fresh tomatoes, if using, and cut them in halves or quarters.
Place in a saucepan with 2 tbsp of water and set over a medium-low heat. Cover and simmer for 10–15 minutes, stirring occasionally, until the tomatoes are soft and their skins have become wrinkled and detached from the pulp.
Purée through a mouli or food mill, discarding the skin and seeds.
In a clean pan, sauté the onion and garlic in the oil until translucent. Add the puréed tomatoes, basil, sugar and some salt.
Simmer uncovered for 20–30 minutes until thick. For a smoother sauce, pass through the food mill again.
Alternatively if using canned tomatoes, drain them, then pass the tomatoes through a food mill or pulse in a food processor. Add to the sautéed onion and garlic and proceed as above.

Roasted bell peppers

Bell peppers are rarely eaten raw in Sicily as they are considered highly indigestible. Even cooked, they can play havoc with the delicate workings of the Sicilian digestive system.

Either impale the peppers with a carving fork and hold over a gas flame for as long as your arm holds out, waiting for the peppers to char and bubble, or roast under a hot grill for about 10 minutes, turning frequently, until the skin starts to blacken and burst.
Put the charred peppers in a plastic bag and leave to cool – this will make the skin easier to remove.
Peel the peppers and discard the seeds and core.

Hand-made maccheroni 'busi'

della Signora Filippa Bartolotta (in her own words)

Even in Sicily, few people make pasta at home anymore, but occasionally it is companionable to sit around a large table, making maccheroni and exchanging gossip, as I did with three generations of Bartolotta women. Rolling the pasta around *busi*, thin, wiry stalks of dried grass, is a time-honoured technique; the modern substitute is a knitting needle.

For 4–6
1kg/2lb4oz semolina flour
1 heaped tbsp salt
½ teaspoon sugar
2 tsp oil

'Warm a pan of water, add slowly to the flour. Add enough to make a stiff dough. Use a big mixing bowl. Some Sicilians use a *scanaturi*, a piece of wood on which you mix the flour on the table top or on your knees. You can mix the dough in a machine but it's better to do it by hand.
Really knead well, keep punching down with your knuckles, turn over, punch down, turn around and over for 15–20 minutes. Add a little water to make it a bit softer but it still needs to be stiff.
Keep turning until all the flour is absorbed. You can tell it's ok if it leaves a hole when you poke your finger in the dough. Work it a bit more until it gets really smooth. Keep going. If it's too smooth, add a little flour, if it's too hard, add a little water.
Cover with a damp cloth and leave for a while.
Take a little bit, roll into a long, thin sausage about 3–4 inches long. Cut into little pieces then roll each one around the stalk or wire until they're 4–5 inches long. The hollow shapes simply slip off the wire, then hang them to dry over the edge of a large basket or bowl.
Eat with tomato sauce, basil, fried aubergines and ricotta salata. You could have no finer dish.'

Fish stock

Makes 1 litre/1¾ pints
750g/1lb10oz fish heads and bones, thoroughly washed
1 onion, sliced
parsley stalks
½ tsp dried thyme
2 bay leaves
250ml/9floz white wine
1 tsp black peppercorns
1 tsp salt

Cover the fish heads and bones with water, add the other ingredients and bring to a rapid boil.
Skim, then turn the heat down and simmer for 20 minutes, skimming frequently. Strain before using.

Home-made ricotta

Either sweeten for use in cannoli and similar pastries, or add a little salt and pepper and serve with dishes of olive oil, olives, capers, pickles, tomatoes and bread. Alternatively, spread on toasted bread and sprinkle with chopped fresh herbs.

Makes about 350g/12oz
750ml/1 pint 7floz goats' or ewes' or full-fat cows' milk
150ml/5 floz double cream
1–2 tbsp lemon juice
½ tsp salt

Heat the milk and cream up to simmering point, then remove from the heat and gradually add the lemon juice, stirring all the time.
Then add salt. The milk should curdle pretty quickly, after which you don't need to add any more lemon juice.
Pour into a colander lined with several layers of damp cheesecloth and leave to drain for at least 1 hour.

Vanilla sugar

Italian housewives are able to buy little packets of vanilla sugar, but you can make your own simply by burying a vanilla pod in a jar of caster or icing sugar.

index

Page numbers in **bold** refer to feature text, page numbers in *italics* refer to photographs

contact details

ALMONDS
Giovanni Pagliarello
Via Roma, 71
Noto (Siracusa)
tel: 0931 835256

BLACK BREAD
La Bottega del Pane di Rizzo Tommaso
Via Garibaldi, 85
Castelvetrano (Trapani)
tel: 0924 81088

BOTTARGA
Conservittica Sammartano
Strada Comunale Maddona 4
Favignana (Trapani)
tel/fax: 0923 921054
www.egadi.com/favoniocsf

CAROB
Karrua
Via Gianforma PM, 81
Modica (Ragusa)
tel: 0932 771791

COFFEE
Torrefazione Termini
Via Napoli, 12
Palermo
tel: 091 334553

FLOUR
Antico Mulino
Via Santa Croce
Longi (Messina)
tel/fax: 0941 485025
www.anticomulino.com

HONEY
La Bottega dell'Ape
Via Cavour, 94
Caltanissetta
tel/fax: 0934 25116
email: caldon@tiscalinet.it

LEMONS
Giuseppe & Ettore Cracchiolo
Via Artale, 174
90045 Cinisi (Palermo)
tel: 091 8695081

LENTILS
Nicola Longo
Contrada Tramontana
Ustica (Palermo)
tel: 091 8449179

MARMALADE & PRESERVES
Azienda Agricola San Giuliano
Ufficio Commerciale
via dei serragli 8
50124 Florence
Italy
tel: 055 2399931
fax: 055 2656461
email: info@disangiuliano.it
www.disangiuliano.it

OLIVE OIL
Angela Consiglio
Via Ugo Bassi, 12
Castelvetrano (Trapani)
tel/fax: 0924 904364

Nicolo Peruzza
Via Circonvallazione
Castelvetrano (Trapani)
tel: 0924 905133
fax: 0924 82313

Girolamo Campagna
Via XX Settembre, 33
Castelvetrano (Trapani)
tel: 0924 89213
fax: 0924 907280

Gianfranco Becchina
Via Trinita
Castelvetrano (Trapani)
tel: 0924 89295
fax: 0924 907540

U Trappitu,
www.esperya.com

Ravidà
Via Roma, 173
Menfi (Agrigento)
tel: 0925 71109
fax: 0925 71180

PASTA
La Corleonese
Via Santa Lucia, 3
Corleone (Palermo)
tel: 091 8463612
www.anticacorleone.com

PEACHES AND BROAD BEANS
Assessorato Agricoltura e Foreste
Via Cavallotti, 6
Leonforte (Enna)
tel: 0935 904655

PISTACHIOS
Antonino Caudullo
Viale Reg Margherita, 132
Bronte (Catania)
tel: 095 7722372
fax: 095 691205
email: caudulan@tiscalinet.it

SALAMI
Consorzio Salame S Angelo
Piazza V Emanuele, 19
S. Angelo Di Brolo (Messina)
tel/fax: 0941 534194
www.salamesangelo.com

TOMATOES
Giacomo Giunta,
Contrada Marina Marza,
Ispica (Ragusa)
tel: 0931 791204

TORRONE
M Geraci
Via Niscemi, 253
Caltanissetta
tel/fax: 0934 581570
www.geraci1870.it

SHOPS
Il Tulipano
Via Vittorio Emanuele, 10/12
Erice (Trapani)
tel/fax: 0923 869672

Pasticceria Palazzolo
Via Nazionale, 123
Cinisi (Palermo)
tel: 0918 665265

Esperya
(For hand-picked Sicilian produce to order via the internet)
www.esperya.com

RESTAURANTS
Antica Focacceria 'S. Francesco'
Via A. Paternostro, 58
Palermo
tel: 091 320264

Nasca 2
Contrada Canna,
Cerda (Palermo)
tel: 091 8992716

Trattoria el Pescador
Piazza Europa, 38
Favignana (Trapani)
tel: 0923 921035

Ristorante 'Al Fogher'
C da Bellia SS, 117
Piazza Armerina (Enna)
tel: 0935 684123
fax: 0935 686705

Ristorante Primafila di Dioniso Munaco
Via B Saputo, 8
Terrasini (Palermo)
tel: 091 8684422
www.sicilian.net/primafila

COOKERY CLASSES
L'Olmo Cookery School
L'Olmo
Via Olmo, 16
Carruba (Catania)
tel: 095 964920
fax: 095 964729
email: ambra_paterno_castello@citiesonline.it

La Cucina del Sole
(di Eleanora Consoli)
Via Contemare, 9
Viagrande 95029 (Catania)
tel/fax: 095 7890116

Diane Seed
fax: 066 797103
www.italiangourmet.com

MISCELLANEOUS
Slow Food
Via della Mendicita Istruita
12042 Bra (Cn)
Italy
tel: 0172 419611
fax: 0172 411218
email: slowinfor@slowfood.com
www.slowfood.com

Rosy's Corner
(for personalised, English-language guiding services)
www.rosy@sicilian.net

Linda Ruggiero
(guesthouse in a 19th century villa in Terrasini)
www.clik.2/villalinda

bibliography

Baratta, Don. *The Sicilian Gentleman's Cookbook* (Prima Publishing, California, 1993)

Barzini, Luigi. *The Italians* (Penguin Books, London, 1968)

Bianchi, Anne. *Italian Festival Food* (Macmillan, New York, 1999)

Carluccio, Antonio & Priscilla. *Complete Italian Food* (Quadrille, London, 1997)

Colonna Romana, Franca. *Sicilia in Boca* (Editrice de 'il Vespro', Palermo, 1974)

Consoli, Eleonora. *Agrumi* (Edizioni Krea, Palermo, 1992)

Coria, Giuseppe. *La Cucina della Sicilia Orientale.* (Franco Muzzio, Padova, 1996)

Del Conte, Anna. *Gastronomy of Italy* (Bantam Press, London, 1987)

Cronin, Vincent. *The Golden Honeycomb* (Rupert Hart-Davis, London, 1954)

Dettore, Maria Paola. *Sapori di Sicilia* (Idea Libri, Rimini, 1999)

Di Leo, Maria Adele. *La Cucina Siciliana* (Newton & Compton, Rome, 1993)
I Dolci Siciliani (Newton & Compton, Rome, 1998)

Field, Carol. *The Italian Baker* (HarperCollins, New York, 1985)
Celebrating Italy (William Morrow and Company, Inc, New York, 1990)
Italy in Small Bites (William Morrow and Company, Inc, New York, 1993)

Fulco. *The Happy Summer Days* (Weidenfeld & Nicolson, London, 1976)

Harris, Valentina. *Southern Italian Cooking* (Pavilion, London, 1993)

Hazan, Marcella. *The Classic Italian Cookbook* (Papermac, London, 1981)

Herrmann Loomis, Susan. *Italian Farmhouse Cooking* (Workman Publishing, New York, 2000)

di Lampedusa, Giuseppe. *The Leopard,* trans Archibald Colquhoun (Harvill Press, 1996)

Lawrence, DH. *Sea and Sardinia* (Penguin, London, 1999)

Longo, Nicola. Unpublished paper for the Comitato Produttori Lenticchia di Ustica

Maggio, Theresa. *Mattanza* (Perseus Publishing, Cambridge, Massachusetts, 2000)

Maw, Mary and Radha Patterson. *A Little Sicilian Cookbook* (Appletree Press, Belfast, 1995)

Middione, Carlo. *The Food of Southern Italy* (William Morrow and Company, Inc, New York, 1987)
La Vera Cucina (Simon & Schuster, New York, 1996)

Pupella, Eugemia Azzolina. *Sicilian Cookery* (Bonechi, Florence, 1996)

Randazzo, Giuseppina. *La Cucina Tipica Siciliana* (Editrice Reprint, Palermo, 1993)
La Pasticceria Siciliana (Antares Editrice, Palermo, 2000)

Risicato, Giuseppe and Palmina. *Risicato's Sicilian Cookery* (Aquila Books, Sydney, 1998)

Robb, Peter. *Midnight in Sicily* (The Harvill Press, London, 1998)

Roden, Claudia. *The Food of Italy* (Chatto & Windus, London, 1989)

Romina, Francesca. *Mangia, Little Italy!* (Chronicle Brooks, San Francisco, 1998)

Sanmarco, Carmelo. *Cucinare alla Siciliana* (Edtrice AR CO, Palermo, 1998)

Schiavelli, Vincent. *Papa Andrea's Sicilian Table* (Birch Lane Press, New York, 1993)

Seed, Diane. *Italian Cooking with Olive Oil* (William Morrow & Company, New York, 1995)

Slow Food, *Il Buon Paese*, (Slow Food Editore, Bra, 2000)

Steingarten, Jeffrey. *The Man Who Ate Everything* (Alfred A. Knopf, New York, 1998)

Tasca Lanza, Anna. *The Heart of Sicily* (Clarkson Potter, New York, 1993)
Malerba A Tavola (Bruno Leopardi Editore, Palermo, 1999)

Taylor Simeti, Mary. *On Persephone's Island* (Vintage Books, New York, 1986)
Sicilian Food (Grub Street, London, 1999)

Tornabene, Wanda and Giovanna with Michele Evans. *La Cucina Siciliana di Gangivecchio* (Alfred A Knopf, New York, 1996)

Valli, Emilia. *La Cucina Siciliana* (Calderini, Bologna, 1997)

Various authors, *In Sicilia In Cucina* (Sigma Edizione, Palermo, 1998)

Wolfert, Paula. *Mostly Mediterranean* (Penguin Books, New York, 1996)

acknowledgements

Clarissa Hyman: I doubt whether this book could have been accomplished without the help of Rosy and Michele Biundo who gave me so much insight into daily life in Sicily, shared many eating adventures with me and welcomed me into their Sicilian family.

I owe a huge debt to the International Slow Food Movement and all members of Slow Food Sicily for their invaluable work in campaigning to support many of the artisan producers featured in these pages. Without the Slow Food Ark that aims to protect endangered foods, this would be a book largely written in the past tense.

I would like to thank everyone at Esperya, a wonderful source of hand-picked Sicilian and Italian foods, especially Alison, Antonio and Tobia, for their help and advice.

The distinguished writings of Mary Taylor Simeti and Anna Tasca Lanza were an immense inspiration, and I am grateful that I was able to draw upon their incomparable experience and understanding of Sicilian culture and cooking.

Thanks to all my family and friends for their support, especially Adrian Gardiner, Chris Johnson and Zena Swerling for loan of resource materials, 'Gero Biundo and Dianne Carroll for help with translation, and Rosemary Barron and Gita Conn for their unflagging encouragement.

Huge thanks to Michele Barlow for recipe assistance, advice and all-round enthusiasm.

Special thanks go to all the Sicilians I met who were so generous in time and spirit in helping me with the research for this book, as well as Alessandra Smith of the Italian Tourist Board who was responsible for getting me to Sicily in the first place.

I must also express my appreciation of Peter Cassidy's evocative photography which captures the heart of Sicily, and thank Maxine Clark for her generously shared expertise, as well as Megan Smith whose design for the book is so in spirit with its content.

Finally, thank you, Jenni, for making me an offer I couldn't refuse.

Peter Cassidy: Thank you to my family and friends in Sicily, who helped me to produce the location photographs. *Mille grazie!* I would also like to dedicate my pictures to the memory of Josephine Martorana.